Ashraf Abu Baker

Semi-Automatic Generation of Three-Dimensional Algorithm Simulations

Ashraf Abu Baker

Semi-Automatic Generation of Three-Dimensional Algorithm Simulations

Algorithm Animation

Südwestdeutscher Verlag für Hochschulschriften

Impressum/Imprint (nur für Deutschland/ only for Germany)
Bibliografische Information der Deutschen Nationalbibliothek: Die Deutsche Nationalbibliothek verzeichnet diese Publikation in der Deutschen Nationalbibliografie; detaillierte bibliografische Daten sind im Internet über http://dnb.d-nb.de abrufbar.
 Alle in diesem Buch genannten Marken und Produktnamen unterliegen warenzeichen-, marken- oder patentrechtlichem Schutz bzw. sind Warenzeichen oder eingetragene Warenzeichen der jeweiligen Inhaber. Die Wiedergabe von Marken, Produktnamen, Gebrauchsnamen, Handelsnamen, Warenbezeichnungen u.s.w. in diesem Werk berechtigt auch ohne besondere Kennzeichnung nicht zu der Annahme, dass solche Namen im Sinne der Warenzeichen- und Markenschutzgesetzgebung als frei zu betrachten wären und daher von jedermann benutzt werden dürften.

Verlag: Südwestdeutscher Verlag für Hochschulschriften Aktiengesellschaft & Co. KG
Dudweiler Landstr. 99, 66123 Saarbrücken, Deutschland
Telefon +49 681 37 20 271-1, Telefax +49 681 37 20 271-0
Email: info@svh-verlag.de
Zugl.: Frankfurt, Goethe-Universität, Diss, 2009

Herstellung in Deutschland:
Schaltungsdienst Lange o.H.G., Berlin
Books on Demand GmbH, Norderstedt
Reha GmbH, Saarbrücken
Amazon Distribution GmbH, Leipzig
ISBN: 978-3-8381-0737-0

Imprint (only for USA, GB)
Bibliographic information published by the Deutsche Nationalbibliothek: The Deutsche Nationalbibliothek lists this publication in the Deutsche Nationalbibliografie; detailed bibliographic data are available in the Internet at http://dnb.d-nb.de.
 Any brand names and product names mentioned in this book are subject to trademark, brand or patent protection and are trademarks or registered trademarks of their respective holders. The use of brand names, product names, common names, trade names, product descriptions etc. even without a particular marking in this works is in no way to be construed to mean that such names may be regarded as unrestricted in respect of trademark and brand protection legislation and could thus be used by anyone.

Publisher: Südwestdeutscher Verlag für Hochschulschriften Aktiengesellschaft & Co. KG
Dudweiler Landstr. 99, 66123 Saarbrücken, Germany
Phone +49 681 37 20 271-1, Fax +49 681 37 20 271-0
Email: info@svh-verlag.de

Printed in the U.S.A.
Printed in the U.K. by (see last page)
ISBN: 978-3-8381-0737-0

Copyright © 2010 by the author and Südwestdeutscher Verlag für Hochschulschriften Aktiengesellschaft & Co. KG and licensors
All rights reserved. Saarbrücken 2010

Dedication

This dissertation is gratefully dedicated to my late loving mother:

Nijme Fuad Aref Hmaidy
(28.06.1990)

Acknowledgements

Although this dissertation is the result of the author's research, without the encouragement and support of some people the completion of this thesis would have been much more difficult, if not impossible. To all those people I would like to express my deepest gratitude, especially to my advisers: Prof. Dr. Detlef Krömker, who granted me the opportunity to launch this research, as well as Prof. Dr. Georg Schnitger for their patience, support and guidance.

I also owe my sincere gratitude to all those with whom I have published a number of useful papers, for their great cooperation: Borislav Milanovic, Dr. Alexander Tillmann, Dipl.-Inf. Stefan Kappes and Dipl.-Inf. Dirk Grunwald.

Publications

Some parts of this research have already been published in several papers. In particular, Section 4.3 draws on the work presented in [13] and [12]. Section 5.5 and 5.7 are based on the research published in [11] and [14], respectively. Two further papers on the visualisation of parallel algorithms and the development of reversible 3D applications were submitted recently to the InfoVis-2009 conference [1] and will not have been reviewed before submitting this thesis. Additionally, four papers were published on topics, not directly related to this research, but to e-learning themes, and are therefore not included in this thesis [17, 16, 15, 121].

Abstract

Algorithms[1] and data structures constitute the theoretical foundations of computer science and are an integral part of any classical computer science curriculum. Due to their high level of abstraction, the understanding of algorithms is of crucial concern to the vast majority of novice students. To facilitate the understanding and teaching of algorithms, a new research field termed "algorithm visualisation" evolved in the early 1980's. This field is concerned with innovating techniques and concepts for the development of effective algorithm visualisations for teaching, study, and research purposes.

Due to the large number of requirements that high-quality algorithm visualisations need to meet, developing and deploying effective algorithm visualisations from scratch is often deemed to be an arduous, time-consuming task, which necessitates high-level skills in didactics, design, programming and evaluation.

A substantial part of this thesis is devoted to the problems and solutions related to the automation of three-dimensional visual simulation of algorithms. The scientific contribution of the research presented in this work lies in addressing three concerns:

- Identifying and investigating the issues related to the full automation of visual simulations.

- Developing an automation-based approach to minimising the effort required

---

[1] The term algorithm derives from "Muhammad ibn Musa Abu Ja'far Al-Khwarizmi", the name of a mathematician and astronomer. He is considered to be the father of algebra and was among the first to use zero as a place holder in positional base notation [75, 74].

for creating effective visual simulations.

- Designing and implementing a rich environment for the visualisation of arbitrary algorithms and data structures in 3D.

The presented research in this thesis is of considerable interest to (1) researchers anxious to facilitate the development process of algorithm visualisations, (2) educators concerned with adopting algorithm visualisations as a teaching aid and (3) students interested in developing their own algorithm animations.

Zusammenfassung

Als fundamentale abstrakte Konzepte der theoretischen Informatik sind Algorithmen und Datenstrukturen ein integraler Bestandteil jedes klassischen Kurrikulums eines Informatik-Studiums. Aufgrund ihrer abstrakten Eigenschaften stellt das Verstehen der Arbeitsweise von Algorithmen für viele Studierende eine große Herausforderung dar. Um das Lernen, Lehren und Erforschen von Algorithmen und Datenstrukturen zu vereinfachen, wurde Anfang der 80er Jahre ein Forschungsgebiet namens Algorithmenvisualisierung geschaffen. Als Teildisziplin der Softwarevisualisierung befasst sich dieses Forschungsfeld mit der dynamischen Visualisierung des abstrakten Verhaltens von Algorithmen und den diesen zugrundeliegenden Datenstrukturen. Algorithmenvisualisierung gilt als ein modernes e-Learning- und e-Teaching-Instrument, das Computergraphiktechniken einsetzt, um das Verstehen, Vermitteln und Erforschen von Algorithmen zu erleichtern.

Ein Hauptziel dieser Dissertation besteht darin, Ansätze zur Automatisierung von dreidimensionalen visuellen Algorithmensimulationen zu entwickeln und zu implementieren. Eine visuelle Simulation eines Algorithmus ist eine interaktive Animation seines Verhaltens und der Zustandsänderungen seiner Daten, der eine Echtzeitsimulation des Algorithmus zugrunde liegt. Der wissenschaftliche Beitrag dieser Arbeit besteht darin, die bislang unerforschten Probleme der vollautomatischen Visualisierung von Algorithmen zu identifizieren und zu analysieren, mögliche Lösungswege und -ansätze zu entwickeln und diese in eine zu schaffende Algorithmenvisualisierungsumgebung zu implementieren. Desweiteren präsentiert die

Arbeit einen Ansatz zur Minimierung des Aufwands für die Entwicklung von visuellen Simulationen paralleler Algorithmen und einen Ansatz zur passiven Animation von Algorithmen zu $\mathcal{NP}$-vollständigen Problemen.

Die Motivation der Arbeit resultiert zum einen aus dem für viele unbefriedigenden aktuellen Stand der Technik, zum anderen aus dem erheblichen Aufwand, der benötigt wird, um lerneffektive visuelle Algorithmensimulationen von Grund auf zu entwickeln und bereitzustellen.

Die Arbeit wird eingeleitet mit einer Einführung in Terminologie und Geschichte der Algorithmenvisualisierung, gefolgt von einem Überblick über repräsentative Algorithmenvisualisierungssysteme und den aktuellen Stand der Forschung. In Kapitel 2 werden die wesentlichen Design- und Entwicklungsaspekte von dreidimensionalen Algorithmensimulationen dargelegt und erläutert. In Abschnitt 2.1 werden Motivation und Notwendigkeit für eine dreidimensionale Visualisierung von Algorithmen erläutert. Aufgrund der zahlreichen Anforderungen, welche von lerneffektiven Algorithmensimulationen erfüllt werden müssen, gilt deren Entwicklung als eine arbeitsaufwendige Aufgabe, die Erfahrung in Didaktik, Design, Programmierung und Evaluation erfordert. In Abschnitt 2.2 werden essentielle Anforderungen formuliert, die die Lerneffektivität von visuellen Simulationen erheblich beeinflussen [95, 99].

Um dem Leser eine klare Vorstellung von der Schwierigkeit des Entwicklungsprozesses zu vermitteln, wurde im Rahmen dieser Dissertation ein Workflow zur Generierung von hybriden visuellen Simulationen entwickelt und in Abschnitt 2.7 vorgestellt. Der Workflow sieht vor, vier Beteiligte in den Entwicklungsprozess zu involvieren: einen Pädagogen, einen Designer, einen Programmierer und einen oder mehrere Evaluierer. Desweiteren wird im gleichen Abschnitt eine Terminologie eingeführt, die es ermöglicht, die einzelnen Bestandteile eines Algorithmus für eine Visualisierung präzise zu spezifizieren und die Komponenten einer Simulation zu charakterisieren. Die Einführung dieser Terminologie war notwendig, um die bei einer vollautomatischen Visualisierung auftretenden Probleme zu charakterisieren.

Abschnitt 2.8 untersucht in wie weit die Entwurfsmethoden Greedy-Algorithmen, Divide-&-Conquer und Dynamische Programmierung die Visualisierungskomplexität von Algorithmen beeinflussen.

Zur Einführung in die Automatisierungsprobleme von Simulationen werden in Abschnitt 3.1 die wesentlichen Unterschiede zwischen Programm- und Algorithmenvisualisierung erläutert. In Abschnitt 3.3 werden zahlreiche Probleme ermittelt und ausführlich dargelegt, die eine vollautomatische quellcodebasierte Visualisierung beliebiger Algorithmen aus praktischer Sicht fast unmöglich machen.

Die identifizierten Probleme werden in Abschnitt 4.1 je nach ihrem Schwierigkeitsgrad in einzelne Cluster unterteilt und anschließend analysiert. Basierend auf der resultierten Analyse wird in Abschnitt 4.2 ein Ansatz zur halbautomatischen Generierung beliebiger dreidimensionaler Simulationen präsentiert. Dieser Ansatz ist eine Kombination aus Vollautomatisierung, Halbautomatisierung und manuellem Eingreifen in den Simulationscode. Der Ansatz wurde umgesetzt und in eine im Rahmen der Arbeit entwickelte Algorithmenvisualisierungsumgebung implementiert. Diese wird in Kapitel 5 vorgestellt.

Aufgrund ihrer enormen Laufzeit lassen sich rechenintensive Algorithmen und Algorithmen zu $\mathcal{NP}$-vollständigen Problemen nicht für Eingaben beliebiger Länge in Echtzeit simulieren. Algorithmen zu Problemen dieser Klasse können nur passiv animiert werden. Bei einer passiven Animation wird der Algorithmus als animierter Film visualisiert, der aus einer konstanten, nicht veränderbaren Folge von visuellen Frames besteht. Im Gegensatz zu einer visuellen Simulation erlaubt eine passive Animation keinerlei Interaktionen, die es dem Benutzer ermöglichen, die Daten des Algorithmus zu verändern bzw. sein Verhalten zu simulieren und somit Einfluss auf den Inhalt der Animation zu nehmen. Der in Abschnitt 4.3 präsentierte Ansatz zur Animation von rechenintensiven Algorithmen und Algorithmen zu $\mathcal{NP}$-vollständigen Problemen basiert auf der Entwicklung einer 3D-Animationssprache und einer Animationsengine (Animationsplayer). Die hierfür entwickelte Sprache verfügt über Elemente zur Modellierung von Datenstrukturen, graphischen Primitiven und zur Erstellung von Komponenten, die von passiven Animationen benötigt werden. Visualisierungen von Algorithmen aus dieser Klasse können in XML-Dateien spezifiziert und vom Animationsplayer abgespielt werden.

Bekanntermaßen stellen sowohl das Lernen als auch das Lehren von parallelen Algorithmen eine große Herausforderung dar. Dies gilt entsprechend für deren Visualisierung. Bei der Visualisierung von parallelen Algorithmen müssen fünf zusätzliche Aspekte berücksichtigt werden, die für parallele Algorithmen spezifisch sind: Synchronisation der verarbeitenden Prozesse, Visualisierung der Kommunikationsmuster, Visualisierung der Kommunikationsroutinen sowie Visualisierung der Datenzerlegung und -zuordnung. In Abschnitt 4.4 präsentieren wir einen clusterisierungsbasierten Ansatz zur Aufwandsminimierung beim Erstellen von visuellen Simulationen paralleler Algorithmen.

Kapitel 4 wird mit einem Abschnitt abgeschlossen, der interessante Visualisierungsaspekte von Computergraphikalgorithmen beleuchtet. Zusammen mit Bioinformatikalgorithmen gelten diese im Allgemeinen als besonders aufwendig zu simulieren.

Kapitel 5 ist der Implementierung der zuvor vorgestellten Ansätze gewidmet. Das Kapitel beginnt mit einer kurzen Vorstellung der im Rahmen dieser Forschung entwickelten und implementierten Algorithmenvisualisierungsumgebung. Diese besteht aus drei Komponenten: Einer Algorithmenvisualisierungsbibliothek, einem Codegenerator und einem Algorithmenvisualisierungssystem namens 3D-Visian.

Der Codegenerator ermöglicht Entwicklern eine halbautomatisierte Generierung beliebiger 3D-Simulationen. 3D-Visian ist eine Algorithmenvisualisierungsplattform, in der beliebige Simulationen und passive Animationen geladen und ausgeführt werden können. Nach einer kurzen Einführung in die eingesetzten Implementierungstechnologien wird der Codegenerator vorgestellt, in dem der in Abschnitt 4.2 präsentierte Halbautomatisierungsansatz umgesetzt wurde. Abschnitt 5.4 stellt einen Mechanismus vor, der entwickelt wurde, um die Anzeige und die Hervorhebung (highlighting) von Algorithmencodezeilen zu automatisieren.

Die manuelle Implementierung einer Undo/Redo-Funktionalität für eine Algorithmensimulation hat sich als eine der aufwendigsten Teilaufgaben erwiesen. Aus diesem Grunde haben wir diesem Problem besondere Aufmerksamkeit gewidmet und die Java 3D API so erweitert, dass sie eine vollautomatische Realisierung von Undo/Redo-Funktionalitäten nicht nur für Algorithmenvisualisierungen, sondern auch für beliebige 3D-Anwendungen, unterstützt. Das zu diesem Zweck entwickelte Konzept wird in Abschnitt 5.5 ausführlich behandelt. Abschnitt 5.7 stellt eine universelle Architektur für das Design und die Implementierung von Algorithmenvisualisierungssystemen vor. Diese Architektur wurde zur Implementierung von 3D-Visian entworfen.

Im letzten Kapitel werden die zuvor vorgestellten Ansätze evaluiert. Das Kapitel wird mit einem Ausblick auf ein zukünftiges Forschungsthema abgeschlossen.

Anhang A enthält Beispielalgorithmen, die in der Arbeit zur Erläuterung von abstrakten Definitionen und Konzepten verwendet wurden. In Anhang B wurden Codeausschnitte aus der Implementierung angehängt. Anhang C enthält eine kurze Einführung in Java 3D.

Contents

Dedication	i
Acknowledgements	iii
Publications	v
Abstract	vii
Zusammenfassung	ix
1 Introduction	**1**
1.1 Terms and Definitions	2
1.2 History of Algorithm Visualisation Systems	5
1.3 Effectiveness of Algorithm Visualisations	8
1.4 State of the Art	11
1.5 Motivation and Objectives	12
1.6 Thesis Outline	14
1.7 Related Work	15
2 Development and Design Aspects	**17**
2.1 2D vs 3D Visualisation	18

	2.2	Features and Requirements	22
		2.2.1 3D implementation	22
		2.2.2 Code listing display	22
		2.2.3 Control points	23
		2.2.4 Collapsible blocks	24
		2.2.5 User interfaces for input and simulation parameter settings .	24
		2.2.6 Direct manipulation	26
		2.2.7 Capturing and displaying of runtime information	26
		2.2.8 Undo/Redo facility	27
		2.2.9 Embedding explanatory text	27
		2.2.10 Documentation	28
		2.2.11 Capturing and export facility	28
		2.2.12 Simplicity and consistency	29
	2.3	Design Aspects of Visual Simulations	29
	2.4	Hybrid Simulations	31
	2.5	Participants (Involved Parties)	32
	2.6	Sample Algorithms	33
	2.7	A Workflow for Constructing Visual Simulations	34
		2.7.1 Steps carried out by the pedagogue	34
		2.7.2 Steps performed by the designer and programmer	40
	2.8	Algorithm Design Paradigms and Visualisation Complexity	48
3	**Towards Automatic Visual Simulations**		**53**
	3.1	Programme Visualisation vs Algorithm Visualisation	53
	3.2	Levels of Abstraction	57

	3.3	Issues and Difficulties	58
	3.4	Conclusions	65
4	**Semi-Automatic Approach**		**67**
	4.1	Problem Analysis	68
	4.2	Semi-Automated Approach	70
		4.2.1	Visual objects	71
		4.2.2	Code augmentation	72
		4.2.3	Reusable parameterised components	73
	4.3	Animation of Computation-Intensive Algorithms and Algorithms for $\mathcal{NP}$-Complete Problems	76
		4.3.1	An algorithm animation language for 3D algorithms	76
		4.3.2	Animating the TSP with xml3DVis	81
	4.4	Visual Simulation of Parallel Algorithms	83
		4.4.1	Parallel algorithms	84
		4.4.2	Visualisation aspects of parallel algorithms	85
		4.4.3	Clustering approach	86
	4.5	Simulation of Computer Graphics Algorithms	90
5	**Implementation**		**91**
	5.1	Implementation Technologies	92
		5.1.1	Abstract Syntax Tree (AST)	93
	5.2	Code Augmentation Techniques	94
	5.3	Code Generator	95
	5.4	Automatic Code Highlighting	97

	5.4.1	Source code-based automatic highlighting	97
	5.4.2	Set-wise code line mapping	99
	5.4.3	Highlighting of pseudo and non-Java code	102
5.5	Automatic Undo/Redo		103
	5.5.1	Undo design patterns	104
	5.5.2	Undo model	106
	5.5.3	Concept fundamentals	106
	5.5.4	Undo/Redo containers	109
5.6	An Algorithm Visualisation Environment		111
5.7	3D-Visian — An Algorithm Visualisation Platform		112
	5.7.1	System Architecture	112

6 Summary, Evaluation and Perspectives 117

6.1	Summary	117
6.2	Evaluation of the Approach	119
6.3	Evaluation of the Approach for Animating Algorithms to $\mathcal{NP}$-Complete Problems	120
6.4	Evaluation of the Undo/Redo Facility	122
6.5	Evaluation of 3D-Visian	126
6.6	Future Work	126

Bibliography 127

Appendices 141

A Sample Algorithms 141

| A.1 | Dijkstra's Algorithm for the SSSP-Problem | 141 |

	A.2 Merge sort	143
	A.3 Red-Black Trees	145
B	**Source Code Listings**	**149**
	B.1 Augmented Code Example	149
	B.2 Python Scanner	152
	B.3 Visual Merge sort	157
	B.4 Visian Comment Parser	162
	B.5 Visual Array	173
	B.6 Undo/Redo Snapshot	185
C	**Miscellaneous**	**191**
	C.1 Java 3D	191

List of Tables

1	An overview of some algorithm and programme visualisation systems	7
2	Requirements for algorithm visualisations and visualisation systems	10
3	Problem overview	68
4	Clustering of the investigated algorithms	89
5	Memory consumption of three distinct applications	123

List of Figures

1	Algorithm, Programme and Software Visualisation	4
2	Snapshots of Sorting Out Sorting	6
3	3D visualisation of Dijkstra's algorithm in JCAT	20
4	Code display	23
5	A snapshot of a selection sort simulation in 3D-Visian	30
6	3D graph editor	43
7	Conceptual structure of a visual simulation	45
8	A visual simulation of a red-black tree in 3D-Visian	46
9	A simulation of a ray tracer in 3D-Visian	47
10	A simulation of Dijkstra's algorithm in 3D-Visian	61
11	A screenshot of a merge sort simulation in 3D-Visian	64
12	Grouping the simulation components based on their creation method	74
13	Semi-automatic approach for creating visual simulations	75
14	Conceptual structure of xml3DVis	80
15	Animation of the TSP in 3D-Visian	81
16	Travelling-salesman problem on a textured sphere created in xml3DVis	83
17	Illustration of an Abstract Syntax Tree	93
18	Structure of the code generator	96

19	A tool for code listing mapping	103
20	Undoable interface hierarchy	107
21	An illustration of the structure of the undo/redo manager	108
22	Container interface hierarchy	110
23	A graphical user interface for C_a	113
24	A graphical user interface for C_b	114
25	A simple illustration of the architecture of 3D-Visian	115
26	A segment of an RNA animation	121
27	Memory consumption of an application with 2300 objects after 100 steps	124

Chapter 1

Introduction

This chapter reviews both, earlier and current research related to the field of algorithm visualisation and algorithm visualisation systems. It is intended to give readers an overview of the topic and make them familiar with this area of research. The first section defines the terminology associated with the topic and describes its relation to software visualisation. Section 1.2 gives a brief history of algorithm visualisation and outlines iconic systems, which have been developed over the past two and half decades. In Section 1.3, we describe a fundamental aspect of algorithm visualisations that determines their didactical quality. A survey of current algorithm visualisations and classical visualisation systems is presented in Section 1.4, followed by a discussion on the motivation behind our research. Finally, we define the goals of this thesis, outline related work, and provide an overview of the organisation of the entire work.

1.1 Terms and Definitions

Visualisation is the process of transforming abstract data into visual representation, in order to simplify understanding of the data's meaning. It is a means of enhancing the visual perception of abstract information. There are three types of visualisations which are of interest to us: information visualisation, scientific visualisation, and software visualisation. **Information Visualisation** focuses on the use of techniques for visualising large-scale non-physically-based data, such as economic and textual or structural information. **Scientific Visualisation** is the visualisation of physically-based spatial data of scientific processes or phenomena, such as geographical and biomedical data, chemical processes, weather simulations, etc. **Software Visualisation** (SV) is the art and science of using computer graphics technologies to generate visual representations of various aspects of software and its development process [49]. SV can be separated into two subfields – algorithm visualisation and programme visualisation. **Programme Visualisation** (PV) refers to mapping the static and dynamic aspects of programmes to graphical representations in order to enhance human's understanding of their actual implementation and structure. **Algorithm Visualisation** (AV) on the other hand, is the process of graphically illustrating the abstract behaviour of an algorithm and the internal changes of the state of its underlying data structures. It uses computer graphic techniques to extract the algorithm's data and operations to produce well-designed graphic representations and animations of these abstractions. AV can be considered as a modern e-learning instrument or technique, which can greatly aid learners to easily understand, and instructors to comprehensively explain the non-trivial behaviour of an algorithm or a data structure. They serve as a powerful supplement or in some circumstances even as an alternative to conventional learning and teaching tools, such as static textbooks, blackboards and transparencies, and thus, contribute to enhancing the quality of education. Not only students and instructors can benefit from this technology, but also researchers and algorithm designers can make use of it to investigate and enhance algorithms and data structures (A&DS)

1.1. TERMS AND DEFINITIONS

and develop new ones. Brown [25] stated "Experimenting with an animation with Knuth's dynamic Huffman trees [78] revealed strange behaviour of the tree dynamics with a particular set of input. This lead to a new, improved algorithm for dynamic Huffman trees [124]. A variation of Shellsort was discovered in conjunction with static colour displays of Bubblesort, Cocktail-Shaker Sort, and standard Shellsort [66]".

There are two kinds of systems related to algorithm visualisations:

- **Algorithm Visualisation Design Tools**, which are constructed to aid the design of new algorithm visualisations; and

- **Algorithm Visualisation Systems** (AVS), which serve as an execution environment to launch and explore pre-designed algorithm visualisations.

In related literature, the term "**algorithm animation**" is widely used to describe any form of animated algorithm visualisation. In our work, however, we distinguish between two distinct types of algorithm visualisations: passive algorithm animations (static animations) — or simply animations, and interactive algorithm animations, hereafter referred to as visual simulations — or simply simulations.

In **a passive algorithm animation** an algorithm is visualised as an animated film consisting of a constant, unchangeable sequence of frames. The animation does not support any user interactions that allow for a modification of the input data, which could consequently influence the behaviour of the animation. The input of the algorithm or the data structure has already been fixed and hard coded by the animation author at the time of creation and can not be modified later. The behaviour of the algorithm or data structure is identical in each run of the animation. Learning commonly takes place by watching the animation film in a passive way.

Visual algorithm simulations on the other hand, are interactive animations with an underlying real-time simulation of the algorithm or the data structure. Unlike passive animations, visual simulations allow users to interactively modify the

4   CHAPTER 1. INTRODUCTION

input data of the algorithm, or access and manipulate the elements of the simulated data structure before or during the execution of the simulation. Furthermore, they support the implementation of various levels of interactions and overcome the limitations inherent in passive animations.

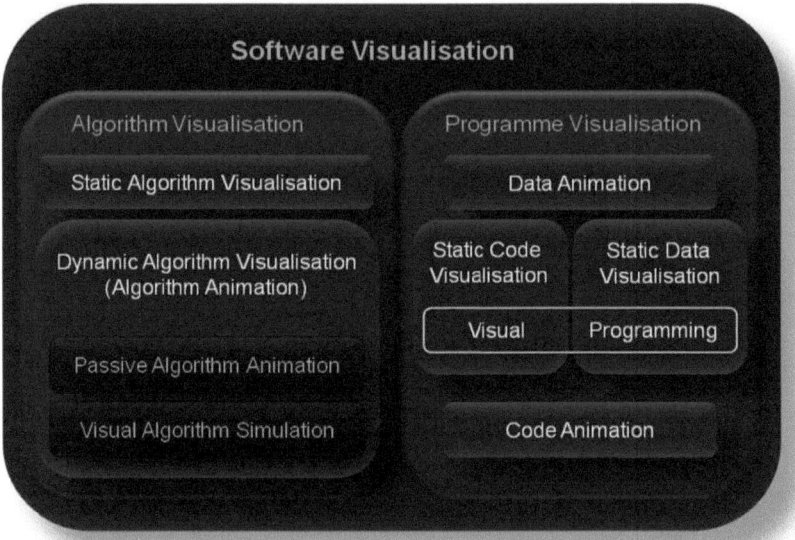

Figure 1: Algorithm and Programme Visualisation as subfields of Software Visualisation

Figure 1 shows the relationship between SV, AV, and PV based on an extension of the taxonomy of Price et al. [91]. The **static algorithm visualisation** in the figure refers to the non-animated presentation of algorithms using formatted text, flowcharts [58], diagrams [85] and images. This approach is widely used in textbooks and transparencies, and is not to be confused with the static animation of algorithms. **Dynamic algorithm visualisation** (algorithm animation) denotes any kind of computer-animated visualisation of algorithms. **Visual Programming (VP)** is a relatively modern approach to creating programmes. The approach seeks to make programmes easier to specify by using a visual notation. In this approach, a developer creates a programme using so called visual programming languages or graphical tools rather than specifying it textually [126].

Although a visualisation is not necessarily animated, in the following, we use the expression "algorithm visualisation" as a generic term to denote both forms of algorithm animations — passive animations and visual simulations. This expression can be understood as a synonym to the term "algorithm animation", which is prevalent in most SV literature.

1.2 History of Algorithm Visualisation Systems

A significant effort on the development of novel algorithm visualisation techniques and systems has been made over the past two and half decades. The computer graphics pioneer Kenneth Knowlton [76] was the first to develop the earliest computer animation language **BEFLIX** [77] in 1963 and to use it to produce bitmap animations of dynamically changing data structures. The history of algorithm visualisations, however, can be traced back to the early 1980's. Probably the first well-known algorithm animation is the thirty-minute film entitled **"Sorting Out Sorting"** [10], which was introduced by Ronald Baecker at the SIGGRAPH conference in 1981. The colour-sound-film introduces nine distinct sorting algorithms and illustrates the differences in efficiency of the various algorithms (see Figure 2).

Afterwards, a large number of algorithm and programme visualisation systems and hundreds of individual visualisations were developed and made available online [109]. In what follows, we briefly introduce some noteworthy representative systems with a special focus on well-known recent systems.

The first two algorithm visualisation systems, which have significantly influenced subsequent systems are BALSA (**B**rown **AL**gorithm **S**imulator and **A**nimator) and TANGO (**T**ransition-based **AN**imation **G**enerati**O**n). **BALSA** [26] is an interactive monochrome algorithm animation system developed by Marc Brown and

6   CHAPTER 1. INTRODUCTION

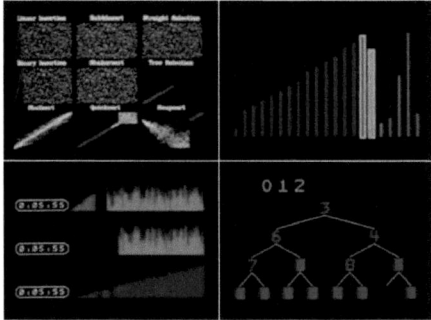

Figure 2: Four snapshots of Sorting Out Sorting [10]

Robert Sedgewick at the Brown University. It provides support to multiple simultaneous views of an algorithm's data structures and displays multiple algorithms, being executed simultaneously. **TANGO** [113] was developed in 1989 by John Stasko also at the Brown University. It introduced the path-transition paradigm, which enables creating smooth and continuous image movement. Further, TANGO introduced a new framework for algorithm animation systems, which has been successfully adopted by many subsequent systems as their fundamental architecture. Both systems have been extended to BALSA-II and XTANGO, respectively. **BALSA-II** was developed in 1988 for Apple Macintosh computers and extended with step and break points, in addition to a number of other features. **XTANGO** [114] is an X-Window version of TANGO, which utilises a path-transition paradigm to produce smooth animations. **POLKA** [90] is a further development of XTANGO and was designed to create concurrent animations for parallel programmes. **SAMBA** is a classical interactive ASCII-based animation system, which served as a front-end of POLKA. The system has a widely used classical architecture, which comprises an animation interpreter that reads graphical ASCII-commands and translates them into corresponding animation actions. **JSAMBA** [71] is the Java version of SAMBA. While SAMBA can run only on Unix and Windows, JSAMBA is platform-independent. More recent and up-to-date systems, which are noteworthy

1.2. HISTORY OF ALGORITHM VISUALISATION SYSTEMS

are ANIMAL, MatrixPro and JHAVÉ [83], all of which are platform-independent systems and are still in use. **ANIMAL** [95, 96] is an algorithm animation system and algorithm animation design tool developed by Guido Rößling. The tool is used to design several types of algorithm and data structure animations. The system is the environment used to play the created passive animations. ANIMAL was developed in Java and introduced several new advanced features, not found in earlier systems. **MatrixPro** [73] is a system designed for instructors to create visual simulations of data structures and algorithms using a flexible drag and drop implementation.

Counting all developed systems would go beyond the scope of this work. Instead, Table 1 gives an overview of some of the algorithm and programme visualisation systems developed so far.

System	Year	Programming Language	Platform	2D/3D
Balsa	1985	Pascal	MacOS	2D
Zeus	1989	Modula	Unix	2D
XTango	1990	C	Unix	2D
UWPI	1990	Pascal	Unix	2D
Pavane	1991	Prolog	MacOS	3D
Polka	1992	C++	Unix	2D
SAMBA	1995	C++	Unix/NT	2D
eliot	1996	C	Unix	2D
CAT/JCAT	1996	Java	platform-independent	3D
GASP-II	1996	Fortran	Unix	3D
Leonardo	1997	C	MacOS	2D
Gawain	1998	Java	platform-independent	2D
JAnim	1999	Java	platform-independent	2D
Algorithma	1999	Java	platform-independent	2D
Jeliot	2000	Java	platform-independent	2D
ANIMAL	2001	Java	platform-independent	2D
JSAMBA	2003	Java	platform-independent	2D
JHAVÉ	2005	Java	platform-independent	2D
MatrixPro	2005	Java	platform-independent	2D

Table 1: An overview of some algorithm and programme visualisation systems

1.3 Effectiveness of Algorithm Visualisations

The ultimate target of any algorithm visualisation is to maximise its learning effect in an efficient way by conveying hidden information regarding the abstract behaviour and the fundamental operations of its underlying algorithm. The effectiveness of an AV is measured by its pedagogical impact or learning effect. The learning effect can be objectively assessed by measuring the increase in knowledge per a given unit of time. A considerable number of independent empirical studies and experiments have been conducted to examine the benefits of AV [65]. Brown, for example, who used BALSA [26] to teach an introductory course in computer programming, has reported that the use of visualisations as an additional teaching aid "has led to demonstrable gains in speed of comprehension". Stasko's students who used SAMBA [112] to study a computer science algorithm course "have enjoyed using the animation. The animation engaged students' creativity and expressiveness and enhanced the students' understanding of the algorithms."

Although further studies [46, 62, 79, 10, 57] have shown similar results, there are some experiments [61, 98, 116], which have concluded that there has been no significant difference between using animations and traditional teaching materials. Hansen believes that the disappointing results in some studies are not due to the algorithm visualisation as a technique, but due to the approach used to convey the visualisations [62]. No doubt, the results of any study are highly dependent upon the quality of the visualisation being used. Nevertheless, in spite of these conflicting results, it is widely perceived that AV can indeed, significantly facilitate the understanding of the fundamentals of algorithms and data structures, shorten the time required to analyse them and thus, improve the entire learning process. To keep this promise, however, AVs need to be pedagogically effective.

The important question which arises at this point is: What constitutes an effective AV and what features should an effective AVS provide? In other words, which characteristics determine the effectiveness of AV?

1.3. EFFECTIVENESS OF ALGORITHM VISUALISATIONS

To be effective an AV needs to meet a large number of requirements: An AV, for example, is effective when it encourages learners to interact with it and engages them actively in the entire learning process. Naps et al. [84] argue "a visualization technology, no matter how well it is designed, is of little educational value unless it engages learners in an active learning activity."

Besides providing a high-level of interaction, there are numerous aspects that have an influence on the effectiveness of the visualisations. Drawing on the work published by Rößling and other researchers [95, 57, 92], Sabi [99] has prepared a helpful table summarising over 40 requirements for AV and AVS, which can be used as a guide for future developments (see Table 2). Rößling [95] has given a detailed explanation of most of them, and therefore we are not going to discuss them further in this work. We encourage interested readers to learn more about these requirements in the cited works.

#	Requirement	General Requirements	Design & Content	Pedagogical Aspects	Interactivity	Anim. Flow Control
1	Platform-independence	•				
2	Internet-independence	•				
3	Easy installation and maintenance	•				
4	Internationalisation	•				
5	Topic overview	•				
6	Integrated auditive and textual explanation		•			
7	Linking to documentation		•			
8	Navigation support		•			
9	Visualisation-wide consistent presentation		•			
10	Usability of the graphical user interface		•			
11	Usage of colour and other graphical representations		•			
12	3D visualisation		•			
13	Highlighting		•			
14	Smooth transitions		•			
15	Focusing attention		•			
16	Adaptable GUI		•			
17	Clarity of the didactical goal			•		
18	Adequate media synchronisation			•		
19	Interesting events			•		
20	Adjustable granularity			•		
21	Small input data sets			•		
22	Predefined interesting input data			•		
23	Adjustable level of difficulty			•		
24	Contact to reality			•		
25	Exercise support			•		
26	Animation export and storage			•		
27	Embedded analysis and comparison			•		
28	Undo/Redo facility			•		
29	Input data manipulation			•		
30	Next step prediction			•		
31	Quizzes				•	
32	Feedback generation				•	
33	Level of detail				•	
34	Creation of user-defined animations				•	
35	Direct manipulation				•	
36	Video player control					•
37	Enabling/Disabling of sound and text					•
38	Animation speed control					•
39	Breakpoints					•
40	Embedded delay points					•

Table 2: Requirements for algorithm visualisations and visualisation systems

1.4 State of the Art

At the time they were developed, all the previously mentioned systems were considered as revolutionary systems, which greatly helped improve computer science education. Nowadays, most of them are either considered outdated, or they are very domain-specific. Meanwhile, the technologies they had applied have become obsolete. Particularly those which are platform-dependent are difficult to install and run due to advances in operating systems and computer technologies. Some of them are not even available anymore. Indeed, advances in computer graphic technologies and hardware have enabled us to develop new and powerful graphic APIs and visualisation tools, both of which have considerably facilitated the development of new algorithm visualisations and systems. Meanwhile, a number of recent visualisations have been developed and provided online. Since the introduction of Java and Flash in 1996 there has been a conspicuous trend in the late 1990's towards developing individual web-based visualisations. A noticeable amount of visualisations has been designed as web-based applications in Java, Flash, SVG [117], X3D [6, 130, 131], and surprisingly in Excel [123]. They range from an individual visualisation of one single algorithm or data structure to collections of visualisations mostly on related topics taught in undergraduate courses. We estimate the number of published visualisations at over 700. In a recent study on the state of the field Shaffer et al. [109] managed to catalogue over 350 distinct algorithm visualisations. According to Shaffer, most existing AVs are of a poor quality and the topic coverage is mostly confined to easier topics, such as sorting, conventional data structures and graph algorithms. Obviously, these seem to be the most popular subjects of visualisations. Visualisations of algorithms in advanced fields such as computer graphics, bioinformatics, cryptography, etc. are under-represented or not even available. Rößling et al. [97] argue "despite the abundance of algorithm visualization tools now available, their promise as a pedagogical tool is largely unfulfilled." Thus, the questions that arise are: Why are most existing visualisations either of poor pedagogical value or largely ineffective? Why have not AVs been satisfactorily adopted in teaching despite the significant effort made so far? The answers to these two questions form the main motivation of our work.

1.5 Motivation and Objectives

Despite the significant effort made so far by a number of researchers and despite the increasing popularity of AVs among learners and educators, algorithm visualisation has failed to catch on as a recognised effective teaching and learning technology in computer science education. This fact explains why many educators and learners still stick to traditional materials such as textbooks and transparencies.

Not surprisingly, people tend to underestimate the effort required for constructing visual simulations. Experience, however, has shown that developing and deploying effective and high-quality AVs can be a difficult and time-consuming task (see Section 2.7). If one examines how much effort is required to implement each feature listed in Table 2 an average developer might need up to a few weeks to design and develop a powerful effective visualisation from scratch. And once the visualisation has been constructed, it still needs to be tested and deployed in order to be capable of running in a suitable environment and to be accessible online.

Taking part in an annual internship at our Department of Computer Graphics [54], 19 students needed roughly two and half months to develop 38 three-dimensional visual simulations of moderate quality, two simulations each. The students stated that the time needed merely to implement an undo/redo facility was twice as much as the time necessitated to develop the rest of the simulation. Postgraduate students working on Master's theses related to this topic reported similar troubles. The difficulties regarding developing visual simulations will be made apparent in later chapters.

Unquestionably, the intricacy of implementing visualisations explains the poor quality of many visualisations. This, indeed, affects the attitude of both, instructors

1.5. MOTIVATION AND OBJECTIVES

and students towards the technique. Additionally, instructors are not truly interested in making so much effort to develop their own visualisations, probably because they lack the time. They are rather interested in ready-made, easy-to-use, enlightening visualisations, which they can use in their lectures to demonstrate their ideas without extra effort. Likewise, students are often neither interested in spending a lot of time looking for adequate visualisations that suit their needs nor to cope with the installation of already found ones. The huge variety of available visualisations makes finding appropriate ones very time-consuming. They are more interested in having access to visualisations that help them master their work faster than with books, rather than wasting their time searching for good visualisations at random; not to mention the time needed to learn how to use them. Furthermore, different visualisation authors have different design styles. Consequently, hopping from one visualisation to another always entails re-adapting to the new design style of the others and requires the user to familiarise themselves with the new visualisation or system.

Apparently, the development complexity[1] of algorithm visualisations and the absence of a comprehensive and widely accessible visualisation system are two issues which have significantly contributed to the failure of algorithm visualisations to be adopted as a recognised teaching and learning technology.

Hence, there is a high necessity for inventing novel techniques and methods for minimising the effort required to create algorithm simulations. Furthermore, there is an urgent need for a globally available algorithm visualisation system. These are the very two issues being addressed in this work. Hence, the primary three goals of our research are:

– To identify the problems related to the full automation of algorithm visualisation.

---

[1] Throughout this work, when we talk about development complexity of visualisations, we mean the intricacy of constructing them. The term is used to express the huge effort required for their implementation. It has nothing to do with the computational complexity of algorithms, known from theoretical computer science.

- To develop an approach towards semi-automating the process of constructing three-dimensional simulations of algorithms and data structures, whereby the ultimate goal is to minimise the total required effort.

- To design and develop a modern universal algorithm visualisation environment for developing, executing and hosting arbitrary algorithm visualisations.

1.6 Thesis Outline

Section 1.7 of this chapter introduces some work related to the automation of programme and algorithm visualisations. The target of Chapter 2 is to make the reader familiar with the development process and to give them a notion of how effective simulations are usually constructed. This is achieved by discussing essential development and design aspects of algorithm visualisations, defining a list of requirements, and presenting a workflow for the development of arbitrary simulations. Furthermore, Chapter 2 also examines whether or not there is a link between the common design paradigms: Greedy-Algorithms, Divide-&-Conquer and Dynamic-Programming, and the visualisation complexity of algorithms.

In Chapter 3 we identify and investigate the issues related to visualising algorithms fully automatically, and show why the full automation of meaningful visual simulations is extremely difficult. This finding has lead us to develop an approach for generating simulations semi-automatically. This approach will be presented in Chapter 4. In the same chapter we go a step further and present an approach for animating computation-intensive 3D algorithms and 3D algorithms for $\mathcal{NP}$-complete problems, which inherently cannot be simulated for arbitrary input length. Furthermore, we present a clustering-based approach for facilitating the development of parallel algorithms and conclude the chapter with a discussion on the simulation of computer graphics algorithms. Chapter 5 is devoted to the implementation of the previously developed approaches. In particular, the chapter introduces an algorithm visualisation environment consisting of a code generator, an algorithm visualisation programming interface, and an algorithm visualisation system termed 3D-Visian. We conclude this thesis with a chapter evaluating the entire work and indicating some topics for future research.

1.7 Related Work

The implementation complexity of effective AVs has induced researchers to think of ways for automating the visualisation process or at least for making it easier.

The most common approach of automation is to develop a domain-specific algorithm animation design tool that can be used to ease the production of passive algorithm animations. Such tools are comparable to general purpose animation tools, such as Flash, with the difference that they are geared to the animation of a narrow range of algorithms. Generating animations is usually accomplished by starting the tool as a GUI-based design environment or as a wizard and providing it with the appropriate parameters. These tools are highly specialised and commonly limited to a narrow domain of algorithms. They are best suited for high school students or in general for persons with poor programming skills. Their outcomes are passive animations with little pedagogical value.

The second approach of automation is to develop domain-specific visualisation systems with embedded knowledge regarding the types of objects and operations prevalent in the domain. As a result, the system provides integrated mechanisms that allow for an automatic visualisation of the objects and the animation of the operations. At any rate, this kind of systems is always limited to a selected collection of algorithms.

Another widely used approach for automation is the on-the-fly visualisation of programme codes [69]. Jeliot3 is an excellent programme animation application that is intended to be used to visualise the way Java programmes are interpreted.

The programme to be visualised is typed or loaded into a source pane. While the programme is being executed, method invocation, variables, expressions, etc. are displayed on the screen. Students can thus follow the step-by-step execution of the programme.

However, as Jeliot, like any other programme visualisation system, visualises low-level programming-language-specific concepts, such as the execution of loops, method invocations and expressions, as well as data changes to variables, arrays, etc., it is unsuitable for simulating the more abstract aspects of an algorithm.

Unfortunately, apart from a few additional works related to programme visualisation, not much work addressing the automation problem has been published. There is also one system called Algorithma [30]. It uses a special pre-defined pseudo code language. Students can use the language to write their own algorithms, which are then automatically executed.

Since we are mainly concerned with creating visual simulations of arbitrary algorithms, all these systems are quite out of the question for us.

Chapter 2

Development and Design Aspects of Visual Simulations

It is often difficult for people who have never developed visualisations on their own, or have never had a look into the code of already implemented ones, to imagine how visualisations gradually evolve. In this chapter we would like to share with the reader our practical experience in designing and developing three-dimensional simulations that we have collected during our research work. Our aim is to give the reader an insight into the development process and highlight its most fundamental aspects. Our primary goal in doing so is to communicate how to construct adaptable[1] simulations that ensure a maximum learning effect and provide a high degree of simplicity and usability. We will first start by illustrating why using 3D graphics in algorithm visualisation is essential and beneficial. Section 2.2 characterises a set of features and requirements which our 'to-be-constructed' simulations are expected to meet, and explain the pedagogical motivation behind each of them. Section 2.3 briefly discusses some design aspects that should be minded when designing algorithm simulations. In Section 2.5, we introduce the parties involved in

---

[1] A simulation is adaptable if it exhibits features that enable the user to adapt it to their level of knowledge, and if it can be turned from a self-study to a teaching simulation and vice versa without intrusion into the source code (see Section 2.4 and 6.6).

the development process and define their individual roles. Finally, we present a workflow for creating visual simulations and assign each step to a particular party involved. The chapter is not only geared to researchers, but also to visualisation designers and developers, such as students who are willing to work on theses related to the topic, as well as to educators who are interested in offering courses or internships concerning algorithm visualisations.

2.1 2D vs 3D Visualisation

The advantages of using the third dimension to produce three-dimensional visualisations are numerous. From a visual point of view, algorithms can be divided into three classes: two-dimensional algorithms, three-dimensional algorithms and augmented two-dimensional algorithms.

Two-dimensional algorithms in the context of visualisation are algorithms that can be satisfactorily visualised in a two-dimensional scene. Visualising them in a three-dimensional space might enhance their beauty and make them look more artistic; though it comes with little or no additional pedagogical benefit. Most well-known sorting, planar graph, and string-matching, polygon clipping algorithms, raster graphics algorithms, etc. fall into this category.

Three-dimensional algorithms in this context are algorithms that can, strictly speaking, only be visualised in a three-dimensional scene. There are many reasons why an algorithm cannot be visualised unless the third dimension is available:

- The algorithm operates on inherent three-dimensional objects. This applies, for example, to three-dimensional shading algorithms and algorithms for hidden surface removal [51].

- The algorithm uses two-dimensional objects located in a 3D space. This applies, e.g., to the algorithm of 3D triangulation [18], the shortest line between two lines in a 3D space [22] and the 3D Voronoi diagram problem [48].

2.1. 2D VS 3D VISUALISATION

- The algorithm works on two-dimensional objects plotted on a two-dimensional plane; however, the operations carried out by the algorithm can only be graphically depicted in a 3D scene. The best example for this is shading a plane by applying a ray tracer where tracing the rays can only be depicted in 3D.

Plenty of examples for 3D algorithms and structures can be found in the field of bioinformatics and computer graphics: Many biological processes can only be simulated comprehensively using 3D. Enzymes, for example, which are large molecules that control particular chemical reactions, are mostly proteins and have a three-dimensional structure, which can only be modelled and rendered using three-dimensional geometry. Any physical interaction between enzymes and the molecules they affect is simulated in 3D. Algorithms for three-dimensional protein folding [122] and RNA structure predicting algorithms [94] are further examples for 3D simulations in bioinformatics (see the animation of the ILM-algorithm in Figure 26).

Computational geometry is a subfield of the computer graphics discipline which is concerned with solving geometrical problems. Most geometrical algorithms in this field are inherently 3D. Examples thereof are: calculating the area of a 3D polygon, delaunay triangulation of a set of 3D points, the 3D surface mesh generation algorithm [72], computation of the convex hull for a set of 3D points, etc.

Much more interesting is the group of augmented two-dimensional algorithms. Obviously, there is no point in using the third dimension in the Graham scan algorithm [125] to compute the convex hull for a set of 2D points. However, there are various advantages of augmenting other 2D algorithm visualisations to 3D. The major purpose in doing so is to use the third dimension to encode additional useful information that can usually not be rendered in 2D. This supplementary information aims to raise the level of expressiveness of the visualisation and to increase the quality and quantity of information conveyed. Algorithms, which fall into this category are called **augmented two-dimensional** algorithms. Examples of augmented two-dimensional algorithms are Dijkstra's algorithm [100, 34], the closest-pair problem [59], and the travelling-salesman problem (see below).

20 CHAPTER 2. DEVELOPMENT AND DESIGN ASPECTS

The approach of using the third dimension to produce three-dimensional visualisation for 2D algorithms has been satisfactorily explored by Brown and Najork [23]. According to Brown there are three distinct applications of 3D:

- Expressing fundamental information about structures that are inherently two-dimensional.

- Uniting multiple views of an object.

- Capturing a history of a two-dimensional view.

We will only discuss the first point using Dijkstra's algorithm, which is, according to our classification, an outstanding example of an augmented two-dimensional algorithm (see Appendix A). Interested readers are encouraged to learn more about the remaining two points in [23].

The main idea behind point one is to augment the 2D data structure of the algorithm to incorporate additional data. Figure 3 shows an animation of the algorithm in JCAT [82].

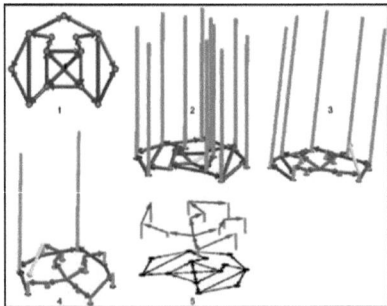

Figure 3: 3D visualisation of Dijkstra's algorithm in JCAT

Image 1 in the upper left corner of the figure shows the initial graph. Each edge in image 2 leaves a vertex at height 0, and enters the other vertex at a height proportional to its cost (distance). The distance associated with each vertex is shown

2.1. 2D VS 3D VISUALISATION

as a green column sticking out of the vertex. The column height is proportional to the cost of the vertex.

Whenever an edge (u, v) is visited to compute the estimated minimal distance from the source node to v, the edge is highlighted in yellow, and lifted by an amount proportional to the distance of u. The edge is lifted so that its start point hits the tip of the green column above u. If the endpoint of the lifted edge is lower than the green column above v, this column is lowered to the endpoint, reflecting the lowering of the distance of v by the algorithm, and the colour of the edge changes from yellow to red (see Image 3). Otherwise, the yellow edge simply disappears (see Image 4). When the algorithm terminates, the graph has been replaced by the shortest path tree. The height of each column above a vertex v reveals the length of the shortest path from the designated source vertex to v. Image 5 shows the graph after the complete execution.

Another example of an augmented 2D-algorithm is the travelling-salesman algorithm [45]. Illustrating the nodes of the algorithm as cities placed on a globe makes the algorithm intuitive and increases the quality of the visualisation, which in turn has a positive psychological impact, thus, leading to an improvement of its didactical quality.

Unfortunately, apart from a few individual 3D visualisations implemented as applets, it seems like there has been very little work done on three-dimensional visualisation of algorithms over the past years; although the importance of 3D visualisation was identified early in 1992. Polka3D [115], and Zeus3D [24] which are further developments of Polka and Zeus, respectively, were the first systems to enable the creation of three-dimensional animations. GASP-II [110] is another algorithm animation system developed in 1997 which allows the presentation and interactive exploration of 3D geometric algorithms over a network. The most recent three-dimensional animation system is JCAT [82], which was developed in 1996 as web-based Java implement of CAT. CAT in turn is a web-based further development of Zeus3D. However, all these systems are, like most other systems of short life or considered antiquated.

Within the scope of our investigation, we were primarily concerned with the creation of three-dimensional visual simulations. The scope of the system we will introduce in Section 5.7, however, is universal in terms of its ability to be used for three-dimensional as well as for two-dimensional simulations and animations.

2.2 Features and Requirements

In what follows, we specify the fundamental requirements of our 'to-be-constructed' simulations:

2.2.1 3D implementation

To further the developments of unconventional algorithms, particularly 3D algorithms in computer graphics and bioinformatics, and not to restrict the scope of the implemented algorithms to two dimensions (see Section 2.1 above), we require that our simulations be implemented using a powerful 3D graphics API. Such simulations are scarce and almost unavailable.

2.2.2 Code listing display

For a student, it is very helpful, if the simulation is accompanied with a textual representation of the algorithm's source code listing, specified in pseudo code as well as in at least one object-oriented programming language. When the algorithm executes a step, the simulation highlights the corresponding code lines in the accompanying code listing display. The learner then can observe which part of the algorithm's code has triggered the most recent visual changes in the simulation. Conversely, they can recognise which visual operation corresponds to which set of

2.2. FEATURES AND REQUIREMENTS

instructions in the code. Nicely formatted code listing using syntax colouring increases the readability of the code and lets the entire simulation look vivid (see Figure 4).

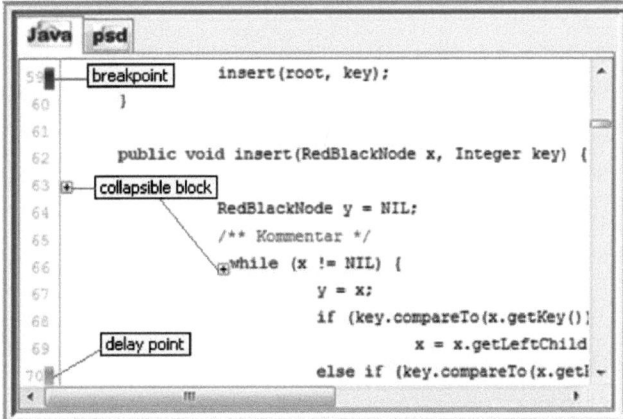

Figure 4: Code listing display, collapsible blocks and control points

2.2.3 Control points

To manage the abstract details of an algorithm, students should be given the option to adjust the granularity of each simulation step and to merge several steps into a single one. The granularity of a step is defined by the number of its contained operations (see Section 2.7.1). This can be achieved best by allowing the user to add and remove break and delay points, and enabling them to convert a **breakpoint** into a delay point and vice versa, all at execution time. When a breakpoint is reached, the simulation suspends its execution and waits until the user prompts it to proceed, e.g., by clicking on the 'resume' button. A **delay point** forces the simulation to delay its execution for a period of time, adjustable by the user. Breakpoints and delay points are termed **control points** (see Figure 4).

2.2.4 Collapsible blocks

A collapsible block is a collection of successive code lines that can be collapsed and expanded at runtime to vary the simulation's level of detail (see Figure 4). Whenever necessary, the learner can vary the simulation's level of detail by hiding or exposing the operations' details of its underlying algorithm. A remarkable aspect of collapsible blocks and control points is that they allow an educator to turn a self-study simulation into a teaching simulation and vice versa simply by making few mouse clicks without the need to intrude into the simulation's source code. Together with control points, they have proven to be an excellent means to make simulations adaptable and to govern the execution of the simulation at runtime.

2.2.5 User interfaces for input and simulation parameter settings

As our goal is to build interactive real simulations rather than passive animations, the user should be given the possibility to customise three kinds of input parameters: the algorithm's input data, the algorithm's conceptual parameters, and the animation parameters. The latter are the configuration parameters of the simulation that do not affect the actual behaviour or flow of the algorithm. An **animation parameter** might be used to control the animation pace or to fine tune its appearance. It may indicate whether a simulation should use spheres/circles or cubes/squares to render the fields of an array. It might also indicate which colour should be used to denote the currently visited path in the DFS algorithm [103, 33], or whether the simulation should prompt the user to answer quizzes or not.

Conceptual parameters are algorithm-specific mostly non-input parameters that affect its behaviour and flow, such as the increment sequence of shellsort [66], or whether quicksort should select its pivot element randomly or always pick the element at a fixed position. A further example is whether a simulation of a volume ray tracer should use BSP tree or Rope tree as a data structure [64]. Furthermore,

2.2. FEATURES AND REQUIREMENTS

they can be parameters for a specific type of simulations such as setting the number of processes for a simulation of a parallel algorithm.

Input parameters are the input data of the algorithm or parameters that affect them. An input parameter, e.g., indicates whether the input set of a sorting algorithm should be generated randomly. Another parameter can be used to indicate the length of the randomly generated input.

The interface should also permit selecting predefined input data, for example, input sets that demonstrate different aspects of the algorithm, such as its worst-case, average-case and best-case behaviour. The viewer can thus observe how a given input set can affect the performance of distinct algorithms solving the same problem. Additionally, the interface should enable the user to restore default values. If the simulated algorithm uses a hierarchical data structure that cannot simply be typed by hand, e.g., a graph, the interface should allow the user to model the data structure in a convenient way. Moreover, it should support them, if necessary, in laying out the modelled data structure automatically.

Note that permitting the user to regulate the animation speed is a further possibility for enabling them to adjust the simulation's level of detail. People obviously learn at different rates. Some learners take longer to capture an algorithm step than others. It is therefore of great importance to allow the learner to set the pace of the animation to a value that fits their individual capabilities. Furthermore, if a learner has comprehended an animated step or a loop, they will prefer in the next run to see its result rather than its details. This can simply be achieved by temporarily setting the animation duration to zero.

The usability aspect of a user interface is also of great importance; any user interface should be quick to learn and easy to use [4, 107]. For this reason, we demand that the design of any user interface comply with well-known usability guidelines.

2.2.6 Direct manipulation

Using the keyboard to perform certain operations on a simulation, such as supplying it with input or changing its conditions is not as convenient as using the mouse. Direct manipulation is a mechanism, which offers the user additional options to interact with the simulation by picking objects directly. It is frequently, but not only, used in computer graphics simulations. Per direct manipulation, one can, for example, specify the clipping area of a polygon clipping algorithm, reposition the light sources of a shading simulation or perform geometrical transformations on objects in a ray tracing simulation. This mechanism may also allow the user of an AVL-tree [103, 111] simulation to explore how a left-rotation or a right-rotation operation works using the mouse and a context menu [129], though doing so might lead to violating the AVL-properties. Note that not every simulation needs to support direct manipulation.

2.2.7 Capturing and displaying of runtime information

Understanding the runtime analysis and the asymptotic behaviour of algorithms is a challenging task, especially for novice students. Not only in theory, but also in practice, it is important to know for a given problem and a particular input set with certain characteristics, which algorithm among all of those that solve the problem is the most efficient one. Consider, for example, sorting algorithms. Due to its average runtime of $\theta(n \log n)$, quicksort is considered one of the fastest comparison-based sorting algorithms. The non-randomised version of quicksort, however, has a miserable runtime when processing a pre-sorted input set, and is slower than bubble sort, which in reality has a bad average runtime of $\theta(n^2)$. Programmers are expected to be aware of this unexpected behaviour of quicksort and such unobvious phenomena. Thus, understanding the runtime behaviour is crucial, not only from a theoretical but also from a practical point of view. Capturing and displaying

2.2. FEATURES AND REQUIREMENTS

runtime information is especially beneficial, if the algorithm simulation system allows executing multiple simulations simultaneously. Using the same input set, the user can run several simulations in parallel, compare their performance and gain a deeper understanding of their runtime behaviour.

2.2.8 Undo/Redo facility

One of the most fundamental and useful aspects of a simulation, which considerably improves its effectiveness, is its ability to support reversing (undoing) and redoing of performed actions. A simulation which does not implement this fundamental feature is likely to fail to hold its promise of being effective. We require, therefore, that our simulations allow the user an unlimited undo/redo of the algorithm's events and the user's actions. Implementing an individual undo/redo facility for each simulation has turned out to be a time-consuming laborious task. In Section 5.5 we will present an automated solution to this problem.

2.2.9 Embedding explanatory text

Mapping the algorithm's state and operations to visual abstractions synchronised with code listing highlighting might not always help the student to capture each activity of the algorithm. Both features should be supplemented with a textual explanation of the operations in action. Each action and each step should be described clearly in a textual form and presented synchronously with the visualisation and the code listing highlighting as an informative narrative. The explanatory text is particularly helpful whenever the viewer fails to take in a step just by watching the visual changes and the code listing highlights. Additionally, as we will see in Section 2.3 and 3.3, a well-designed simulation typically uses a specific colour encoding to efficiently convey information regarding the current state of its underlying algorithm. Explanatory text can be used to clarify the association between the colours and the algorithm's states.

Note that teaching simulations usually do not need explanatory text as the instructor can provide a better explanation than a simulation projected on the wall.

2.2.10 Documentation

We require that our simulations provide access to offline and online hypertext documentation. A documentation can possibly include an introductory tutorial on the algorithm and, if necessary, a simple manual on how to run the simulation and interact with it.

2.2.11 Capturing and export facility

This feature is intended to be used by educators to prepare their teaching materials, and is a requirement for the visualisation system rather than for the simulation itself. A powerful algorithm visualisation system is typically implemented as an online or a stand-alone application, which can be readily linked to any presentation materials used by an educator. In order to demonstrate a simulation of an algorithm live in a lecture, the educator initially needs to navigate to the location of the visualisation system, launch it, select the simulation from a repository, and finally, enter the input data and set animation parameters before they can start the demonstration. This procedure lasts too long to be performed live in a lecture. It additionally needs a prior training and may fail if unexpected technical troubles suddenly emerge. Alternatively, the educator can perform the procedure prior to their lecture and use the capturing feature to record each step, and subsequently export the recording in a platform-independent format that they can incorporate into their teaching materials. This feature can additionally enable the educator to create manuscripts and digital hypertextbooks [21] for their courses, containing passive algorithm animations.

2.2.12 Simplicity and consistency

Simplicity and consistency are two key design aspects of visual simulations that significantly affect the user's acceptance, and the effectiveness of a simulation. "Simplicity" means that each simulation should be as easy to use and as quick to learn as possible while preserving a high degree of effectiveness. A superior simulation is an enlightening one which not only offers a maximal learning effect, but is also straightforward to learn and to use. Consistent design means that all simulations ought to be designed in the same style, and consequently communicate with the user in the same manner. From a user's perspective, it is not worthwhile reading long manuals just to learn how to use a simulation or a simulation system. For this reason, simulations should be designed in such a way, that once the user has learned how to handle one, they should be able to know how to deal with all others. Indeed, this can easily be achieved if simulations are implemented and designed in the same visualisation context (visualisation system).

Other requirements that are frequently demanded in the literature are in our opinion taken for granted and will not be explicitly discussed in this work. These include: incorporation of a control panel to control the flow of the simulation, using smooth animations, supporting a high degree of interactivity, etc.

2.3 Design Aspects of Visual Simulations

Obtaining uncomplicated and easy to use simulations necessitates employing a consistent design throughout all simulations. This entails a uniform use of colour and graphical primitives, a uniform animation style, and a uniform interface design. In what follows, we discuss these four design aspects:

- Uniform use of colour
  A well-designed simulation usually uses a colour encoding to communicate

with the user. A colour encoding assigns a specific colour to a set of simulation objects reflecting their current state. When a simulation is being executed, the data upon which the algorithm operates is logically partitioned into three parts: the part which has finally been processed, the part being processed, and the part which still needs to be processed. One simple way to denote each of these three parts is to assign a unique colour to each one. For example, one can use gold, red and grey to denote the already sorted elements, the elements being sorted, and the unsorted elements of a sorting algorithm simulation, respectively. A uniform use of colour means in this case that once the designer has decided to use, say grey to mark the unsorted elements, this colour should be adopted for marking these elements in all other sorting simulations. Figure 5 shows a snapshot of a selection sort simulation in which each data part is coloured as described above. Additionally, the portion of the array being currently processed is denoted using a rectangular border. This colouring scheme has been adopted for all sorting algorithms.

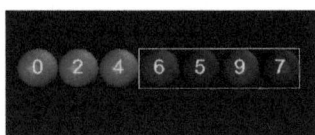

Figure 5: A snapshot of a selection sort simulation in 3D-Visian

- Uniform use of graphical primitives

  It is also of big importance that different algorithm simulations sharing the same data structures consistently use the same visual representation for these structures. That is, simulations should use identical geometrical shapes and appearance for similar data structures. For example, once an array has been modelled as a sequence of 3D spheres, this design style should be adopted for all simulations using arrays.

- Uniform animation

Consistent animation means that identical actions or events of different simulations should be animated in the same manner independent of the underlying algorithm. If a visual comparison of two elements is implemented, say by shaking the elements or letting them blink simultaneously, then this implementation should be applied to all simulations using comparisons. Likewise, animated objects should always move along the same path when demonstrating the same event. This allows the learner to instantly recognise a repetitive event and associate it with its corresponding algorithm step.

- Uniform use of graphical interfaces
  All simulations that expect the same input type or format should employ the same input interface. The same applies to the simulation's control interface.

2.4 Hybrid Simulations

We distinguish between two types of simulations: **self-study** and **teaching simulations**. The main characteristic of self-study simulations, which are basically intended to be used by students, is that they are implemented at a low level of abstraction. That is, they expose the individual low-level details of the algorithm's behaviour and state. Teaching simulations, on the other hand, are implemented at a higher level of abstraction. Depending upon how abstract they are, they hide the individual details of the behaviour of their underlying algorithm. A teaching simulation of, e.g., a parallel algorithm will not visualise how the processors process the tasks assigned to them, but will rather show the results of the computation. A self-study simulation, on the other hand, would do so.

A hybrid simulation is a simulation that can work in both modes (self-study and teaching mode) and can be readily switched from one mode to the other without any intrusion into its code. We seek to realise hybrid simulations.

2.5 Participants (Involved Parties)

In this section we present a classification of the parties involved in the development of simulations and give a description of their individual roles.

Each simulation has the ambition of communicating knowledge to the viewer in an efficient way. As producing simulations which serve this purpose assumes a broad spectrum of knowledge in various fields of computer science and education, we recommend involving four parties in the development process: a pedagogue, a designer, a programmer and evaluators. The **pedagogue**, who ideally is an experienced educator, is responsible for developing a didactical concept that precisely specifies the pedagogical goal of the simulation and describes how it can be achieved. Among others, they specify the fundamental elements (operations and data) of the algorithm that are to be rendered, subdivides the algorithm into logical steps, and specifies where break and delay points are to be set. They predefine well-conceived input data sets that reveal various phenomena of the algorithm and allow the user to freely explore its aspects. Each simulation has a default setup, i.e., default values for the input and the animation parameters (see Section 2.2.5) which should be appropriately set by the pedagogue. Strictly speaking, all simulation aspects that have an effect upon its didactical quality should be conceived by the pedagogue or at least under their direction.

Designing simulations is an artistic challenge, which should be carefully carried out by a competent **designer**. The role of the designer is to sketch effective design concepts for the system and the simulations. They consult the programmer how to visualise the various aspects of the algorithms and how to model and render the data structures in a consistent style. In particular, they define how a simulation can visually communicate with the viewer and always keep their attention focused on the region currently being processed. A well-designed simulation will increase the user's desire to learn.

An experienced **programmer** with advanced programming skills is responsible for providing a stable, extensible, portable and bug-free implementation of the system and the simulations, with respect to the design guidelines proposed by the designer, and the pedagogical aspects. Separating the design from the programming role allows the programmer to primarily concentrate on the programming task. This increases the performance and the stability of the implementation.

Finally, both the system and the simulations should be 'certified' by **evaluators** who are possibly end-users. Their key task is to inspect the simulations for correctness, effectiveness as well as consistency. They also check the system for usability, stability and suitability. Further, they identify possible weak spots, report conceptual and programmatic shortcomings, and make suggestions for improvement.

Strictly speaking, simulations and simulation systems should be conceived, designed, implemented and evaluated by professionals, not by inexperienced programmers. Our proposal for the individual roles does not exclude that one and the same person may assume more than one role, i.e., the programmer and the designer might be the same person.

2.6 Sample Algorithms

As software visualisation is a discipline of the practical computer science, it is not always straightforward to describe the aspects of the visualisation process using precise formal definitions. For this reason, and in order to increase the comprehension of this thesis and to decrease its level of abstraction, we will often introduce informal definitions and explain them using concrete algorithms as explanatory examples. The algorithms that we will frequently use for this purpose are Dijkstra's algorithm, merge sort and red-black trees. As we prefer not to assume that the reader is familiar with the details of these algorithms, we briefly introduce these algorithms and highlight their fundamental aspects. The introduction of these three algorithms is attached to Appendix A. Readers would be well-advised to learn about the algorithms before proceeding with reading the remainder of this work. We have thoughtfully chosen the algorithms above all for the following three reasons:

- They cover numerous aspects of our approach to solving the problem of automation.

- They are quite good representatives of four classes of algorithms: graph algorithms, sorting algorithms, recursive algorithms and trees.

- As they are usually taught in undergraduate courses of computer science, we assume that someone who is reading this thesis has come across them or at least heard of them.

2.7 A Workflow for Constructing Visual Simulations

Although a vast number of research studies on algorithm visualisations have been conducted and published, the details of how an algorithm simulation systematically is built, has not been satisfactorily exhibited. In the following, we define the steps of a workflow for the development of algorithm simulations and assign each step to one of the participants involved in the development process. The implementation details will not be covered here, but rather left to Chapter 5.

2.7.1 Steps carried out by the pedagogue

Step 1: Identifying the fundamental data objects

The fundamental **data objects**[2] of an algorithm are exclusively data objects that are subject to visualisation. From a visualisation perspective, we classify the data objects of an algorithm into **primary** and **secondary** objects. The former are the

---

[2]When we talk about the data objects of an algorithm, we mean all kinds of data upon which the algorithm operates. They vary from simple variables or hierarchical data structures to three-dimensional objects used in computer graphics or bioinformatics.

2.7. A WORKFLOW FOR CONSTRUCTING VISUAL SIMULATIONS

data objects of the algorithm upon which the essential operations of the algorithm act, and should therefore be rendered. The secondary data objects are objects that may or may not need to be visualised. This is because rendering these objects not always leads to an enhancement in understanding the algorithm. In some cases, they should not be visualised as they might distract the learner and could therefore contribute to reducing the learning effect of the simulation. Secondary data objects are mostly auxiliary objects used temporarily to perform particular subtasks or operations. It is the task of the pedagogue to decide whether or not the visualisation of a particular secondary data object will contribute to an increase of the didactical quality of the simulation.

Primary objects are, for instance, arrays used in sorting algorithms, graphs utilised in graph algorithms or trees used in tree algorithms. In general, an algorithm has at least one primary, and anywhere from none to several secondary data objects.

Accordingly, the primary data object of Dijkstra's algorithm is the input graph G; for merge sort it is the input array A; and for a red-black tree it is the tree itself.

The secondary data objects of Dijkstra's algorithm are the priority-queue Q, the distance array d and the predecessor array Π. Note that Q does not need to be visualised at all. The same applies to the predecessor array, which is not even contained in the simulation code. This is because the predecessor of a node in a visual graph can be identified immediately. As can be seen in the visualisation of the algorithm in Figure 10, the estimated distance of a node is labeled on the node. Thus, there is no need at all to visualise the distance array.

In merge sort, we used the pile-metaphor to explain how the merge procedure works. In the implementation of the algorithm, the piles correspond to the auxiliary subarrays L and R (see line 3 in listing A.5). According to our classification, these subarrays are secondary data objects. A simulation at a high level of abstraction, which commonly hides a large part of the algorithm's details, would not render them, while on the contrary a less abstract simulation with more details would.

Red-black trees have no secondary data objects.

Step 2: Identifying the fundamental abstract operations

We will now cover this topic in depth, due to its importance.

The behaviour of an algorithm is determined by the collection of the abstract operations accessing and modifying its underlying data objects. An **abstract operation** in turn is a sequence of low-level actions (code instructions) that the algorithm executes to perform a certain task. Akin to the fundamental data objects, the fundamental operations of an algorithm are those abstract operations which should be visualised, and thus, constitute the entire visual activities of the simulation. There are two types of abstract operations: atomic and compound operations. An **atomic** operation is an algorithm operation that cannot be further broken into smaller ones. A **compound** operation is made up of a collection of atomic or a mixture of atomic and compound ones.

The atomic operations of merge sort are:

1. Splitting the array into two subarrays

    This operation results from the recursion call of the algorithm at lines 3 and 4 of listing A.4:

    $MERGE\text{-}SORT(A, p, q)$;

    $MERGE\text{-}SORT(A, q + 1, r)$;

    This operation was visualised by depicting the resulting subarrays below their parent (see merge sort visualisation in Figure 11).

2. The assignment operations at lines 5 and 7 that copy a field value from the split subarray into its corresponding pile:

    $L[i] \leftarrow A[p + i - 1], \ R[j] \leftarrow A[q + j]$.

    This operation has been animated by having the field value fly smoothly to its target field in the pile.

2.7. A WORKFLOW FOR CONSTRUCTING VISUAL SIMULATIONS

3. The compare operation at line 13, which compares the two top elements of the piles prior to copying the smallest of them into the sorted array:
   if $L[i] \leq R[j]$

4. The assignment operations at lines 14 and 16, which copy an element from a pile into the sorted array as a result of the comparison operation:
   $A[k] \leftarrow L[i]$, $A[k] \leftarrow R[j]$

5. The field access operations at lines 8 and 9

The only compound visual operation of merge sort is the merge procedure.

As for Dijkstra's algorithm, apart from the implementation effort needed to visualise and lay out a directed graph, this algorithm is one of the most straightforward algorithms to visualise. Once the graph has been rendered and correctly laid out, there are only two fundamental atomic operations to animate:

1. Adding the vertex with the minimum distance to S:

   $u \leftarrow \text{ExtractMin}(Q), S \leftarrow S \cup \{u\}$

   We visualise the set S by assigning a uniform colour to all its members along with the edges connecting them. Hence, we illustrate the insertion of a vertex v to S by assigning v and (u, v) the same colour that the elements of S have.

2. Highlighting the adjacent nodes of the recently added vertex v:

   for *each vertex* $v \in Adj[u]$ *do Relax(u, v, w)* (see listing A.2)

   This is achieved by simply highlighting all of the adjacent nodes along with every edge connecting them with v using a predefined colour.

Updating the distances inside the relax procedure is a computational operation, which does not need to be visualised. Figuring out how the minima are updated is not essential for understanding how the algorithm works. The student basically needs to see its result, not how it is computed. Note that the values of the minima are labeled on their corresponding nodes. Any value changes will be visually reflected automatically.

As for red-black trees, the compound operations of the *delete* procedure are:

Finding the successor, the *delete-fixup* routine and the *delete* operation itself. Finding the successor s of a node x can be simply visualised by highlighting the search path from x to s. Thus, this method has two atomic operations: highlight a node and highlight an edge. The *delete-fixup* operation comprises two interesting atomic operations: *leftRotate* and *rightRotate*. Understanding how they work is a requisite for comprehending red-black trees.

Note that the level of abstraction that a simulation is based on, will determine which operations should be visualised (see Section 3.2). Simulations at a low level of abstraction such as self-study simulations normally visualise atomic operations. Simulations at a higher level of abstraction, such as teaching simulations, usually omit the visualisation details of atomic operations. Instead, they depict compound operations that consist exclusively of atomic ones. A simulation at a much higher level of abstraction, such as a teaching simulation, might only display compound operations that are composed of other lower-level compound operations.

Note that an algorithm may include operations that do not need to be visualised or should not even be visualised. Consider, for example, the interval scheduling problem described in [105] and [38]:

Given n tasks and one processor, each task has a start time t_i and a finish time f_i, and thus the time interval $[t_i, f_i]$; two tasks are compatible if their intervals do not overlap; find a maximum subset of mutually compatible tasks.

A simple algorithm, which solves the problem starts by sorting the input tasks according to their finish time. The algorithm subsequently executes the task i that has the minimal finish time provided, and then removes i and each task j with $t_j \leq t_i$ from the task list. The algorithm repeats this step until the task list is empty. Note that the initial sorting step is irrelevant for understanding the algorithm and should not be visualised.

Furthermore, not all fundamental visual operations can be derived directly from

2.7. A WORKFLOW FOR CONSTRUCTING VISUAL SIMULATIONS

the algorithm's source code. Consider the red-black tree. Each *delete* or *insert* operation may affect the geometrical structure of the tree and consequently prompts the tree to be redrawn or laid out again. The layout operation is a visual operation that has no matching instructions in the source code.

Additionally, there are visual operations, which increase the quality of the visualisation, but are not directly contained in the code: Consider selection sort as a second example. At each step i the array is separated into two subarrays: the sorted subarray $A[1, i-1]$ and the unsorted one $A[i, n]$. Step i selects the minimum in $A[i, n]$ and exchanges it with the element $A[i]$. From a didactical point of view, it is helpful to set the sorted subarray apart from the unsorted one by highlighting at least one of them differently. This can be achieved, for instance, by framing the subarray as in Figure 5. Indeed, this visual operation also has no corresponding operation in the code.

Highlighting the pivot element of quicksort is a further example of a visual operation that has no match in the source code.

Step 3: Defining logical steps and setting collapsible blocks

Any algorithm simulation should be logically subdivided into several logical steps. From a visual point of view, a step is a collection of an arbitrary number of atomic or compound operations, or both. The granularity of a step is defined by the number of its enclosed operations and is dependent upon the abstraction level of the simulation. Obviously, a step of a self-study simulation typically has a lower granularity than the steps of teaching simulations. Hence, a teaching simulation of an algorithm often has fewer steps than a self-study simulation of the same algorithm. We mark the start and the end of a step by surrounding it with breakpoints (see Section 2.2.3). A breakpoint simultaneously marks the end of a step, and the start of the following one. Note that giving the user the flexibility to set, remove and convert control points at runtime allows them to refine a step by splitting it into several ones. Conversely, the user can coarsen the granularity of steps by merging several steps into a single one.

In addition to defining the logical steps, we need to set the bounds of each collapsible block. The way in which we combine several operations into a single step has a great impact on the pedagogical effectiveness of the simulation and should be well thought out by the pedagogue.

Step 4: Defining interesting input data sets and default parameters

Step 5: Identifying the algorithm's operations that affect the runtime of the algorithm

Step 6: Preparing the explanatory text

The pedagogue needs to prepare the explanatory text to display when a step is being executed. If any colour encoding is being used to focus the attention of the viewer on certain parts of the simulation, this encoding should also be explained and presented at the beginning of the simulation.

Step 7: Preparing quiz questions

We do not demand that our simulation should implement quizzes. However, if a simulation is to be equipped with its own quiz interface, the pedagogue needs to conceive and prepare meaningful questions [63].

2.7.2 Steps performed by the designer and programmer

Note that one of the most challenging aspects when constructing visual simulations is designing the graphics portion of the visualisation. What follows are the steps carried out by the programmer and the designer.

2.7. A WORKFLOW FOR CONSTRUCTING VISUAL SIMULATIONS

Step 1: Implementing the algorithm in a high-level programming language

Step 2: Designing and implementing a visual presentation of the fundamental data objects and operations

This step additionally involves implementing mechanisms that enable disparate data structures to communicate with each other. We call these mechanisms bridges. Let us consider, for example, a simulation that utilises a visual array and a visual matrix. Suppose, at a particular step during execution, that we need to visualise an array element assignment to a field in the visual matrix. As both visual structures are of different types, we need to implement a bridge that allows both of them to visualise this assignment.

Step 3: Providing pseudo code listing and a simplified implementation of the algorithm in at least one object-oriented programming language

These implementations will be shown in the code listing display each in a separate tab.

Step 4: Designing and implementing a code listing display with an integrated syntax colouring facility

The display should allow the setting of control points and defining collapsible blocks as required in Section 2.2 under Point 2.2.3 and 2.2.4. See also Figure 4.

Step 5: Implementing a code listing highlighter

A code listing highlighter is a programme that maps each step of the simulation to its corresponding code lines in the code listing display, and highlights them at the very beginning of a step.

Step 6: Designing and implementing a narrative manager

A narrative manager is the component used to display the explanatory text.

Step 7: Implementing an undo/redo facility that enables the user to undo and redo the algorithm's performed actions[3] and operations

This step has turned out to be quite laborious. This explains why many visualisation systems provide no support for this fundamental feature. For this reason, we devoted this problem a special attention and developed an automated solution. We will return to it in Section 5.5.

Step 8: Designing and implementing a graphical user interface for conceptual and animation parameters

Step 9: Designing and implementing an input interface for the creation and selection of input data sets

Depending on the input type of the algorithm, this step might imply the implementation of a powerful input tool, such as a graph modelling editor. An input interface may also need to provide an export and import facility for saving and editing generated input structures using platform-independent formats, such as XML [132]. Figure 6 is a screenshot of the 3D graph editor [20], which we employ for modelling input graphs.

---

[3]Actions are performed by the user; operations are conducted by the algorithm.

2.7. A WORKFLOW FOR CONSTRUCTING VISUAL SIMULATIONS   43

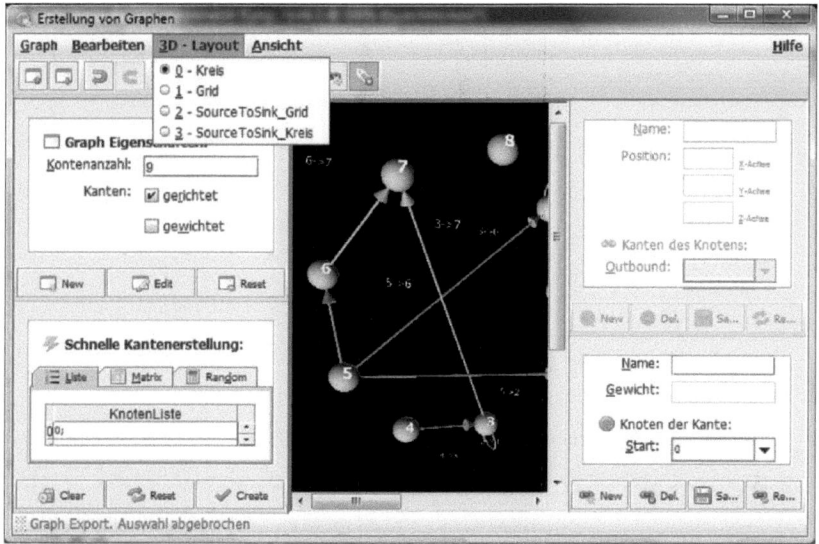

Figure 6: 3D graph editor

Note that input and conceptual parameters should often be set prior to running the simulation. Some visualisation-specific parameters can be set while a simulation is running. The interface should be able to handle both cases.

Step 10: Implementing input validation functions and tools

The prior two steps entail the implementation of input validation functions that read the input data and check it for validity and constraints. Additionally, we need to provide a means for modelling structured input data, especially graphs. As we know, some graph algorithms expect graphs with specific properties. Dijkstra's algorithm, e.g., expects a connected directed graph with positive weights. The Floyd-Warshall algorithm [35], on the other hand, allows negative weights but no negative-weight cycles. Other algorithms expect acyclic graphs. A powerful graph editor, which can be applied as an interface for constructing graphs will certainly allow the user to model graphs with arbitrary properties. Hence, the user might produce a graph whose properties violate the expected ones. In this case, the input data interface must provide validation functions that check the graph for validity and constraints and alert the user in case they are about to launch the simulation on meaningless or incorrect input. A good data input interface is one that restricts in advance the possibilities for entering or creating invalid input.

Step 11: Implementing an error manager

A simulation should implement an error manager to capture user's input errors and view them on a special error display. For example, when the user creates invalid input, the simulation should alert them and give an explanation why the input is inaccurate. If a simulation crashes due to an implementation bug, the error manager collects all necessary information regarding the current state of the simulation that enables tracking the cause of the error, and reports it immediately to the simulation developer to fix it.

Step 12: Implementing a facility for capturing and displaying runtime information

Step 13: Implementing quiz interface

Step 14: Implementing a simulation control panel

This is the interface with which the user can govern the flow of the simulation (start, stop, pause, backward, etc.). Note that this work can be deferred to the implementation of the visualisation system and does not need to be implemented individually for each simulation.

2.7. A WORKFLOW FOR CONSTRUCTING VISUAL SIMULATIONS

Step 15: Implementing additional components

In addition to the features listed above, a simulation may need to implement its additional individual features. For example, a complex simulation, which is also not so straightforward to adjust, might need to provide an animated introduction or a demo.

The figure below shows the structure of a typical simulation. The simulation core includes the source code of the simulation. All other rectangular components (coloured in blue) are graphical components. Oval components represent non-graphical components

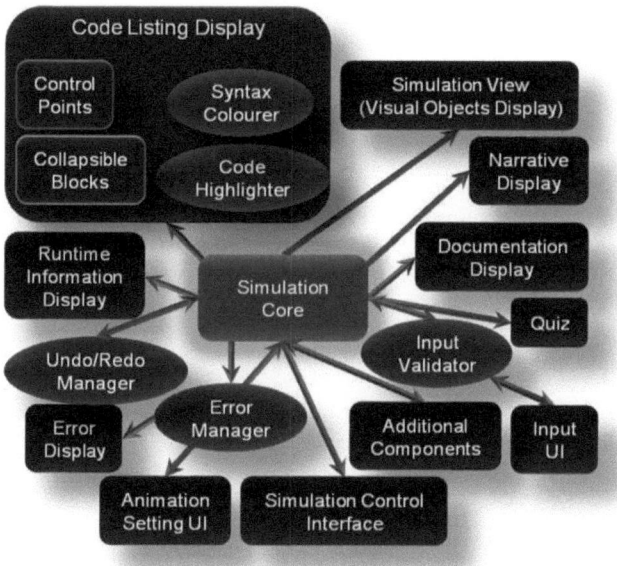

Figure 7: Conceptual structure of a visual simulation

We do not request a simulation to implement its own capturing and export facility as required in 2.2.11. This work can also be shifted away to the visualisation system.

46 CHAPTER 2. DEVELOPMENT AND DESIGN ASPECTS

From the steps above, one can infer how much work and experience is required to produce a useful simulation. The work needed for evaluating the simulation, developing an algorithm visualisation system, making the system available online and accessible from everywhere has not been mentioned yet. As pointed out earlier in Chapter 1, our belief is that the intricacy of implementing such simulations is the main reason for the poor quality of many visualisations available online. This fact forms one of the key motivations to launch this research.

The following figure shows a simulation of a red-black tree in 3D-Visian (see Section 5.7).

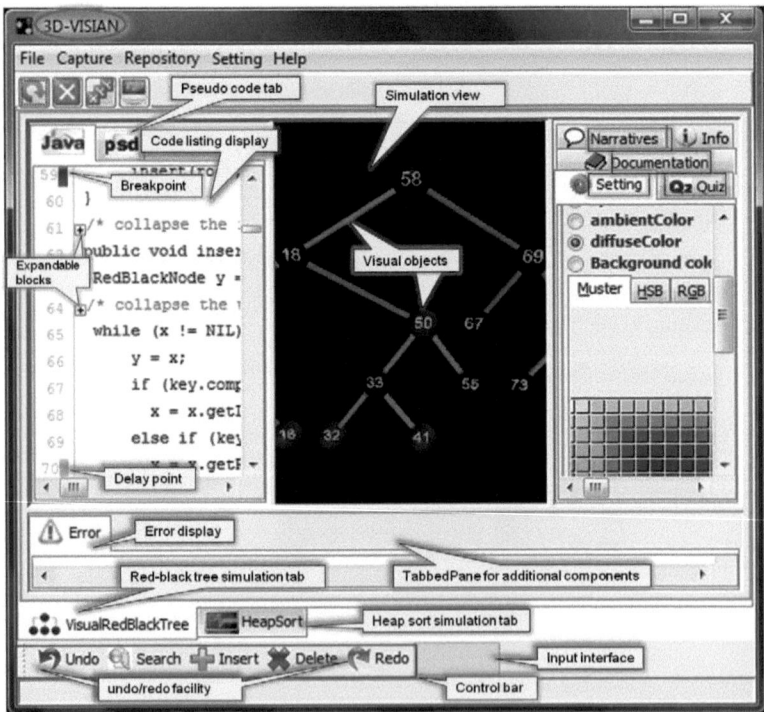

Figure 8: A visual simulation of a red-black tree in 3D-Visian

2.7. A WORKFLOW FOR CONSTRUCTING VISUAL SIMULATIONS 47

Figure 9 shows a ray tracing simulation.

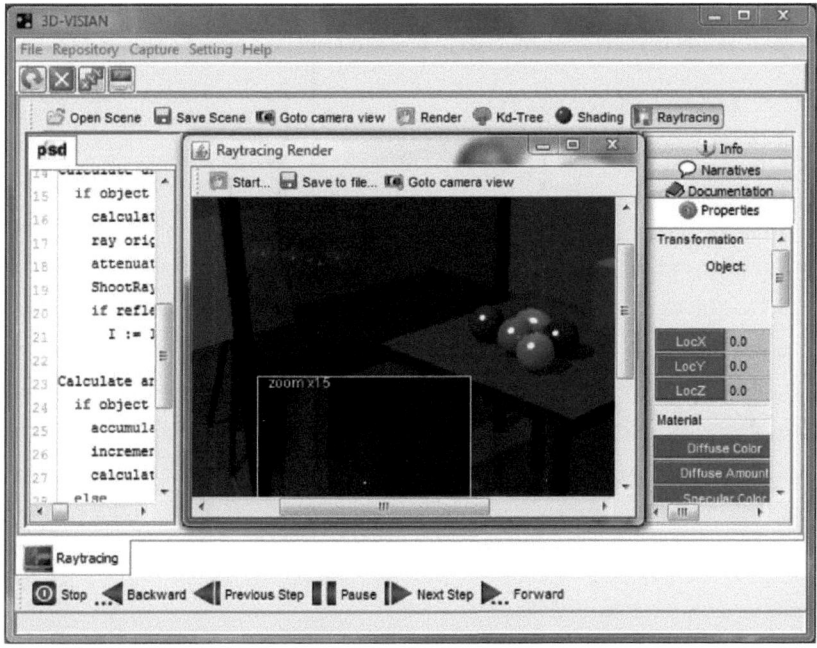

Figure 9: A simulation of a ray tracer in 3D-Visian

2.8 Algorithm Design Paradigms and Visualisation Complexity

In this section we investigate the relation between design paradigms (techniques) and the visualisation complexity of algorithms. In particular, we address the question whether algorithm design techniques can affect the visualisation complexity or not. That is, given different algorithms that solve the same problem and are implemented according different design paradigms. Does the visualisation complexity differ from one algorithm to another? The answer to this question is important when educators who are supervising programming internships on algorithm visualisations wish to distribute the algorithms to the students in a more fair measured way.

Algorithm design paradigms are design methods that can be utilised to develop optimising solutions for problems to obtain an improvement in their computational runtime. We are mainly concerned with three well-known paradigms: Greedy-Strategy, Divide-&-Conquer and Dynamic-Programming.

Algorithm designers apply the greedy-strategy when the algorithm has at each stage a sequence of choices that it can select from. A greedy-algorithm always makes the choice that looks best at the moment. It attempts to construct an optimal solution by repeatedly making the 'best' feasible choice. A solution that has already been taken into the solution set is never given back. Greedy-algorithms may not always yield optimal solutions, yet they are often straightforward to understand and to implement. Examples of greedy-algorithms include Dijkstra, Huffman-code [36], Prim and Kruskal algorithm [104, 44].

The divide-&-conquer strategy is a recursive top-down approach that divides the problem into smaller ones, solves them recursively and combines the computed solutions into a complete one. Well-known divide-&-conquer algorithms are quicksort

2.8. ALGORITHM DESIGN PARADIGMS AND VISUALISATION COMPLEXITY

and merge sort.

Dynamic-programming is a bottom-up approach, that breaks up a problem into smaller (overlapping) subproblems. The smallest subproblems are explicitly solved first; their results are then used to construct solutions of progressively larger subproblems. Dynamic-programming algorithms generally solve a problem in a more compact sophisticated way and are therefore more abstract and generally difficult to understand. They are, however, straightforward to implement. Typical examples for dynamic-programming-algorithms are Matrix-multiplication [41], Floyd-Warshall algorithm [35], and polygon triangulation.

In order to explore the relationship between the design paradigms and the visualisation complexity, we examined a set of algorithms that can be implemented, once according to the brute-force method, and once according to one or more of the design techniques presented above. We next compared the effort required to produce each visualisation separately. The problems investigated were the following: the coin exchange problem (greedy), string matching problem (divide-&-conquer) [43], matrix multiplication (dynamic-programming) [41], longest common subsequence problem (dynamic-programming) [40] and polygon triangulation (dynamic-programming). For the same problem, the investigated brute-force algorithm always uses the same types of operations used by the other algorithms and naturally the same data structures. All the algorithms only differ in the manner in which they approach the solution. A brute-force algorithm solves a problem in the simplest and apparent way. A dynamic-programming algorithm does it in a more sophisticated manner. It 'carefully thinks' which part of the input is best suited to be accessed or modified prior to accessing it. A greedy-algorithm is normally "short-sighted" and acts in a less sophisticated manner than a dynamic-programming algorithm. This fact, however, affects the order in which the operations are performed, yet not their type. In other words, a brute-force, a greedy and a dynamic-programming algorithm when solving the same problem always perform the same operations, yet, in a different order. From a visualisation point of view, reordering the visualisation operations of an algorithm does not affect its visualisation complexity. Consequently, using greedy or dynamic-programming has no significant impact on the complexity of visualisation.

On the other hand, a good visualisation of a divide-&-conquer algorithm will often depict the entire recursion tree and illustrate each recursion step visually. This makes divide-&-conquer algorithms slightly harder to visualise due to issues related to properly layouting the recursion tree. This is especially true when the recursion tree cannot be computed prior to the termination of the algorithm as is the case with recursive randomised algorithms.

From the last discussion, one can infer that the implementation complexity of a simulation is highly dependent on the data structures used, as well as its visual operations. Apart from the effort required to understand an algorithm before it can be simulated, trivial algorithms that are straightforward to understand are not necessarily easier to simulate than those which are much more abstract and difficult to comprehend. It turned out that algorithms, which use tree data structures, such as AVL-trees and red-black trees, (a,b)-trees, HuffmanCode, Heapsort, etc. were the most difficult to simulate among conventional algorithms. This is because they require implementing specific layout algorithms. The more an operation affects the structure of a tree and the more dynamic it is, the more difficult is its implementation.

Graph algorithms also require the implementation of layout algorithms. However, many graph algorithm operations are static in the sense that they do not affect the structure of their graph(s).

Non-recursive sorting algorithms and linear data structures, such as stacks, lists and queues, are the easiest to visualise.

Recursive algorithms require more work, when the visualisation of the recursion tree is desired.

In general, simulations that support direct manipulation and lot of dynamics,

2.8. ALGORITHM DESIGN PARADIGMS AND VISUALISATION COMPLEXITY

movements and repositioning of visual objects have proven to be the most difficult to animate. These are typical visualisation characteristics for many computer graphics and bioinformatics algorithms. This fact may be an explanation why Shaffer et al. [109] found catalogue 134 visualisations of sorting algorithms, but only 57 visualisations of search trees and no visualisations of computer graphics algorithms.

Chapter 3

Towards Automatic Visual Simulations

The objective of this chapter is to identify and examine the issues that arise when trying to visualise simulations fully automatically. We begin by contrasting the ways of how humans and machines tend to perceive programmes and algorithms, and illustrate how this influences the visualisation process. After a short introduction into the theme 'levels of abstraction' in Section 3.2, we reveal a set of key problems that aggravate the automatic visualisation of algorithms. This chapter acts as a preamble for Chapter 4, where we will introduce an approach for generating simulations semi-automatically.

3.1 Programme Visualisation vs Algorithm Visualisation

Programme visualisation encompasses the extraction and visualisation of information regarding the static and the dynamic aspects of a programme. Depending upon the goal[1] of the visualisation, one or more of the following distinct aspects of a programme can be visualised:

- Code
- Structure
- Data
- Execution

The first aspect concerns the visualisation of the programme's **source code listing** by presenting it in a textual form, well-laid-out and well-formatted for human reading.

The second aspect refers to the visualisation of the programme's **structure**, which is defined by the programming-language-specific entities and their associated relationships. Programme entities are variables, expressions, loops, data structures, methods, classes[2], etc.

The programme's **data** is determined by the values of its corresponding data objects. In essence, the state of a programme is defined by the occupancy of these data objects.

The **execution** aspect relates to the dynamic behaviour of the programme at runtime. Visualising the behaviour of a programme typically includes mapping the programme's state to a graphical representation and illustrating how expressions and method invocations constantly transfer the current state of the programme into a new one.

In addition to the four aspects above, programme visualisation is often used for illustrating general programming concepts and showing the programme's control flow. Programming concepts include call trees, recursions, loops, conditional

---

[1] Programmes are mostly visualised for the purpose of teaching, analysing, debugging or testing.

[2] In the remainder of this work we will often use the terminology of the object-oriented programming paradigm when describing programmes' or algorithms' units.

3.1. PROGRAMME VISUALISATION VS ALGORITHM VISUALISATION

statements, etc.

From a machine's point of view, each **algorithm** is nothing else than a programme consisting of a sequence of instructions. This sequence entails a mixture of field declarations, type definitions and method invocations that access the fields and modify their values. From a user's point of view, however, an algorithm is a high-level abstraction of a programme containing a set of abstract data structures and abstract operations. Akin to a programme, an algorithm has a **state** determined by the collection of the values of its underlying data objects. The behaviour of an algorithm is determined by the set of operations it performs upon its underlying data objects.

In general, the basis of a programme visualisation entirely differs from that of an algorithm visualisation. We now highlight the fundamental differences using a practical example:

SelectionSort1(A[1..n])	SelectionSort2(A[1..n])	SelectionSort3(A[1..n])
1 for $i \leftarrow 1$ to $n-1$	1 for $i \leftarrow 1$ to $n-1$	1 for $i \leftarrow 1$ to $length[A]-1$
2 do $next \leftarrow i$	2 do $next \leftarrow i$	2 do $min \leftarrow findMin(A,i)$
3 for $j \leftarrow i+1$ to n	3 for $j \leftarrow i+1$ to n	3 swap(A,i,min);
4 do if A[next]>A[j]	4 do if A[next]>A[j]	4
5 $next \leftarrow j$	5 $next \leftarrow j$	
6 $e \leftarrow A[i]$	6 swap(A,i,next);	**findMin(A[1..n],i)**
7 $A[i] \leftarrow A[next]$		1 min=i
8 $A[next] \leftarrow e$	**swap(A[1..n],i,j)**	2 for $j \leftarrow i+1$ to $length[A]$
	1 $temp \leftarrow A[i];$	3 do if (A[min] > A[j])
	2 $A[i] \leftarrow A[j];$	4 min $\leftarrow j$
	3 $A[j] \leftarrow temp;$	5 return min
		swap(A[1..n],i,j)
		1 $temp \leftarrow A[i];$
		2 $A[i] \leftarrow A[j];$
		3 $A[j] \leftarrow temp;$

Listing 3.1: Selection sort listings

Listing 3.1 includes three distinct code listings representing the selection sort algorithm [106, 111]. They all differ in their level of abstraction, which increases from left to right. The way a human reader grasps this algorithm will differ in the manner in which a machine (computer) interprets it. The left listing illustrates how a machine may capture the algorithm. For a computer, the previous algorithm is a programme containing an array, two nested loops and an *if*-clause. A computer does not know that the inner loop detects the minimum of the subarray $A[j..n]$, nor that the last three code lines constitute a *swap* operation. Furthermore, a computer "with a standard degree of intelligence" would not identify the left code listing as an implementation of a sorting algorithm. From the machine's point of view, the fundamental instructions used in this programme are: variable declarations, variable assignments, array field accesses, and array field assignments; all of which are interpreted as instructions at a low level of abstraction which cannot be further disassembled.

On the other hand, a human reader will tend to capture the given programme in a more abstract way. That is, a human does not see the programme as a sequence of low-level instructions but as one that performs $n-1$ **steps** on an **abstract data structure** (array). In each step, it processes a portion of the array, **compares** elements to each other and **selects** a particular element in the array. At the end of each step the programme **exchanges** the first element of the subarray with the recently picked one. A human reader with moderate or elementary programming skills is likely to recognise the last three assignments as an implementation of a **swap** operation, while a computer would not. After a closer look at the inner loop, they might identify it as an implementation of the "**findMin**" method.

Therefore, when we compare the way a computer interprets a programme to how a human attempts to understand it, we will often conclude that the human's perception of programmes is based on aggregating several instructions (actions/events) into one abstract operation, rather than seeing it as a sequence of elementary instructions. In the example above, these abstract operations are: **compare, find minimum,** and **exchange** (see the words in bold). Furthermore, a human tends to think in terms of abstractions that correspond to real-world concepts or objects, such as step and minimum. These very abstractions constitute the artefacts of a typical algorithm visualisation. As a result, the artefacts of an algorithm visualisation are high-level abstractions of operations and data objects, rather than low-level instructions and programming-paradigm-specific constructs, as is the case with programme visualisation. For this reason, algorithms are commonly taught at higher levels of abstractions than programmes.

As we will see in Section 3.3, the fact that humans and machines have different views of programmes and algorithms, and use distinct levels of abstraction to capture them, fundamentally affects the followed visualisation approach, and consequently determines to what extent the visualisation process can be accomplished automatically.

3.2 Levels of Abstraction

Any programme or algorithm visualisation is grounded upon a certain level of abstraction. In terms of the terminology used in Chapter 2, the level of abstraction determines the artefacts (the abstract operations and objects) of the visualisation. The higher the abstraction level of a visualisation, the more abstract are its artefacts. We denote the level of abstraction on which a given programme or algorithm visualisation is based, by **programme level** or **algorithm level**, respectively.

Note that there can be more than one algorithm level for the same visualisation and that the distance between the programme level and an algorithm level varies depending upon the purpose of the visualisation. A visualisation of insertion sort for teaching purposes will probably hide the details of the *findMin()* method and thus resides at a higher level of abstraction than a self-study visualisation.

3.3 Issues and Difficulties

Visualising both the dynamic and static aspects of a programme can indeed be accomplished fully automatically. The static structure of the programme and its entities can be directly derived from the source code. This is possible, in particular, because all potential entities of a programme are well-defined in the programming language. Furthermore, the types of potential dynamic changes of each programme entity are limited as well. A variable, for example, can be allocated, accessed, modified and deallocated. A method can be loaded, entered, executed, exited and perhaps uploaded but not modified. The changes that constitute the dynamic behaviour of the programme can be inferred from the runtime environment and traced back by monitoring the values of the programme's data. Thus, it is possible to map the code, the structure, the data and the dynamic changes of a programme to static and dynamic views automatically. The main challenge here is more often than not to arrange the corresponding views on the screen due to its limited size.

Unlike programme visualisation, the automatic visualisation of algorithms is problematic and cannot be accomplished without the availability of additional information regarding the abstractions used in the algorithm. As mentioned earlier, an algorithm is essentially visualised by rendering its high-level abstract operations and objects. Often these are not directly denoted as such and can not always be deduced automatically from its source code. We have investigated a large number of algorithms in regard to the possibility of visualising them automatically, and identified, among others, the following problems:

Problem 1: Identification and visualisation of fundamental abstract operations

On top of all the problems associated with automatic visualisation is the determination of the instructions that comprise a particular operation. Usually, to automatically visualise a certain operation, a visualiser (visualising engine) should

3.3. ISSUES AND DIFFICULTIES 59

be capable of identifying all its constituent instructions. This might be possible for common operations, but not generally. One can, for example, encapsulate the instructions of the *findMin* operation of selection sort or the *swap* operation of a sorting algorithm into a method, which can be readily identified. Even though the visualisation remains a problem. Visualising the *swap* operation is namely data-structure-dependent. That is, swapping two array elements visually differs from swapping two matrix or two nodes of a tree structure. As a result, to fully automate a *swap* operation, a visualiser is expected to identify the corresponding code instructions, recognise the data structure being used and implement the visualisation accordingly. This is, however, not feasible for arbitrary data structures.

Let us additionally, consider a red-black tree. How can a visualiser be made to recognise a left-rotate operation [39] as such? Or, how can it identify a ray tracing operation of a ray tracer, which is typically included in the algorithm's code as a linear equation system whose solution computes the intersection of a line with the surface of the object being ray traced [52]?

Beyond that, there are visual operations that have no corresponding instructions in the algorithm's code such as the layout operations of some tree structures.

Problem 2: Identification of primary and secondary data objects

A similar problem applies to the abstract data objects of an algorithm. How can a visualiser distinguish between the primary and secondary data objects of an algorithm? Even if it could, how would it decide which of the secondary data structures should be visualised and which should not? Recall from Section 2.7.1 that a primary data object always needs to be visualised, but a secondary object may or may not need to. It is clear that a visualiser cannot anticipate this just based on the source code.

Problem 3: Identification of access semantics

A visualisation typically employs different methods to communicate with the viewer and to signalise that a certain data object is being accessed. One of the most effective and therefore most used methods to indicate an access is object-highlighting. Whenever an object is being accessed, it is highlighted using a particular colour that depends on the semantics of the access. Consider, for example Dijkstra's algorithm. After initialisation, the nodes of the graph are accessed at four different locations in the code (see listing A.3):

- at line 5 when computing the node with the minimal estimated distance:
  $u \leftarrow EXTRACT - MIN(Q)$

- at line 6 when the node with the minimal estimated distance is removed from V and added into S:
  $S \leftarrow S \cup \{u\}$

- and finally at line 7 and 8 before and inside the **relax**-procedure:
  for each vertex $v \in Adj[u]$
  $doRELAX(u, v, w)$

Thus, the same access operation has, depending on its location in the code, three different contextual semantics, each of which should be indicated using a distinct colour (see Figure 10 below). How can a visualiser recognise which access has which semantics and decide accordingly how to treat it? Furthermore, there are accesses to nodes at other locations that should not be visualised (for example, accesses inside the initialisation routine). How can a visualiser identify which access should be visualised and which should not?

Problem 4: Focusing attention

One way to help the user comprehend a step is to call their attention to the part of the simulation currently being processed. There are two ways to achieve this:

3.3. ISSUES AND DIFFICULTIES

- Encoding the state of the algorithm's data.

- Highlighting the area of interest.

Encoding the state of an algorithm's data is usually accomplished by using distinct colours denoting the portion of data which has been, is being or has not yet been processed. In Dijkstra's algorithm, for example, we use the following colour encoding: Nodes and edges that have not yet been finally processed are grey. All nodes and edges of the shortest path are permanently coloured in gold (see Figure 10). During the relax step, whenever the shortest distances of the adjacent nodes of a node u are being updated, all these nodes, and the edges connecting them with u are temporarily highlighted in red. After the relaxation, all adjacent nodes except the one that has recently been added to S turn grey. From the visualisation in Figure 10, one can see that S contains two nodes, and that the node being relaxed is the upper left one.

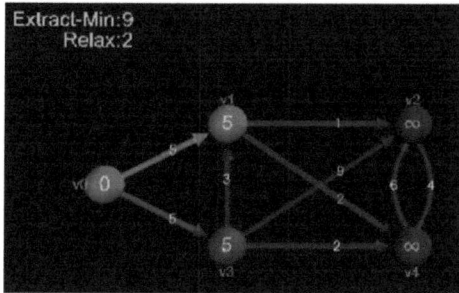

Figure 10: A simulation of Dijkstra's algorithm in 3D-Visian

To highlight the area of interest, one can draw two-dimensional frames around the data objects or fill small regions with transparent colours (see Figure 5).

The major problem with focusing attention is that a visualiser cannot define a reasonable colour encoding and determine the area of interest on its own. Furthermore, it cannot infer from the algorithm's code when temporarily highlighted data objects should be unhighlighted, or when the area of interest changes. Hence,

Problem 5: Cloning data objects

Rendering the recursion tree of a recursive algorithm is necessary to gain a better understanding of the simulation in particular, and to understand the concept of recursion in general. To render the recursion tree, however, a simulation often needs to clone parts of its data objects. Consider for example, merge sort. The partition step of the algorithm, which subdivides the array into two subarrays, is demonstrated by cloning both subarrays and rendering them underneath their parent[3] (see Figure 11 below). The information to clone the partitions of the array is, however, not explicitly included in the source code of the algorithm. This presents a problem for the visualiser.

Note that the need to duplicate data objects is not restricted to recursive algorithms. Consider for example, insertion sort. Initially, before the i-th step starts, the algorithm creates a copy of the array element at position $i + 1$, and assigns it to a variable called 'key' [106, 37]. It then compares the key to the elements of the sorted subarray $A[0..i]$ in order to pinpoint the position at which the key is to be inserted. To visualise the key, the simulation needs to clone the $(i + 1)$-th element of the array (see simulation of insertion sort at [2]). Here too, the instruction to duplicate the element is not explicitly contained in the source code of the algorithm and cannot be identified by a visualiser.

Problem 6: Computation of geometrical coordinates and layout information

Problem five leads to a further one. Before a visual data object can be rendered, the simulation must compute its geometrical coordinates to know where to place it. The

---
[3] Note that the recursion tree does not need to be rendered for every recursive algorithm. There are simulations of recursive algorithms that do not need to clone any of their data objects. An example for this is the recursive algorithm for computing the convex hull [32].

3.3. ISSUES AND DIFFICULTIES 63

data objects of an algorithm, however, generally do not include such information. Therefore when modelling a data object as a visual object, the latter is assigned default geometrical coordinates that appoint its default position in the scene. However, when visual objects of the same type are dynamically created at execution time, as is the case with the subarrays of merge sort, the simulation is forced to compute their appropriate positions at runtime, otherwise they will overlap. In this case the default coordinates are meaningless and unhelpful.

Similarly, hierarchical data structures, such as trees and graphs do not store layout information required to lay them out properly. Using default hard-coded layout values will not suffice, particularly if the data structures change dynamically. Thus, the problem requires implementing specific layout algorithms. However, there are various layout algorithms, each of which is mostly tailored to a specific layout problem. How can a visualiser anticipate which layout algorithm is geared for which structure?

Furthermore, the alignment of visual data objects in a scene has, in particular, in computer graphics algorithms, a great impact on the quality of the visualisation. Arranging objects in a visual scene randomly may result in a meaningless alignment of these objects.

Hence, automatically computing meaningful geometrical coordinates and layout information for arbitrary algorithms is quite problematic. This is particularly true if the algorithm uses dynamically changing structures or objects.

Problem 7: Displaying conceptual information

It is common that a simulation displays additional information that increases the understanding of the algorithm, but this usually cannot be directly derived from the source code. The merge sort simulation, e.g., depicts the number of the recursion step on the right corner of each subarray as can be seen in Figure 11. Likewise, the merge step is indicated by a red arrow which appears above each subarray. A

64 CHAPTER 3. TOWARDS AUTOMATIC VISUAL SIMULATIONS

simulation of quicksort or Dijkstra needs to denote the pivot element or the start node, respectively. Showing additional useful information will no doubt ease the understanding of the algorithm. However, as the information is not included in the algorithm's source code, this process can definitely not be automated.

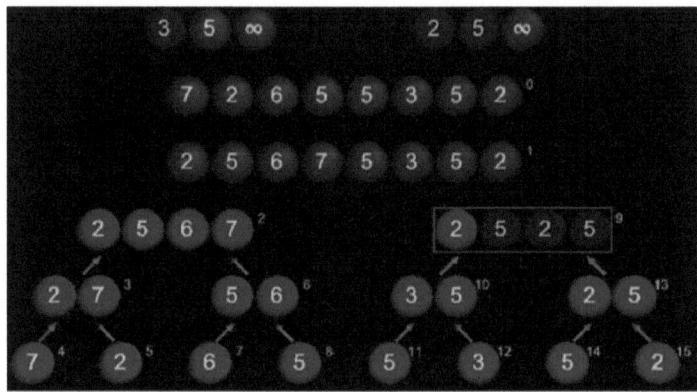

Figure 11: A screenshot of a merge sort simulation in 3D-Visian

Problem 8: Extracting runtime information

Visualising the runtime information of an algorithm is crucial for understanding its efficiency. A convenient way to visualise the runtime information of an algorithm is to depict the exact number of performed key operations at the end of each step. The determination of the key operations, however, differs from one class of algorithms to another. Whereas the key operation of comparison-based sorting algorithms is the compare operation, we usually count the number of visited nodes along the traversing path, when analysing the performance of tree data structures. To automate the visualisation of runtime information, a visualiser should be able to automatically extract this information by identifying the key operation(s), which is particularly difficult when the algorithm performs various kinds of operations.

Problem 9: Defining logical steps

As mentioned earlier, the way in which we separate an algorithm into logical steps has a great impact on the effectiveness of the simulation. For this reason and because subdividing an algorithm into reasonable logical steps requires knowledge regarding the semantics of the operations, this task cannot be reasonably automated.

Problem 10: Mapping data objects to visual objects

Different simulations using the same data object may use distinct visual representation to depict it. Almost each simulation of a sorting algorithm operating on an array renders the array as a sequence of same visual objects, such as spheres. A heap sort visualisation also operates on an array, but additionally uses a 'heap-tree' as a view of the array.

Similarly, consider the 3D bin packing [111] and the 3D convex hull algorithm [32]. At programme level, the input of both algorithms is given as a set of triples. That is, the volume of an object in the bin packing algorithm and a point of the convex hull problem are given as a volume (height, width, depth) or as a point (x,y,z), respectively. A simulation of the bin packing algorithm, however, is likely to use 3D boxes to visualise the bins; and the points of the convex hull are usually rendered as points or tiny spheres in a 3D space. Hence, different simulations may apply distinct views of the same data object. The question is: How can a visualiser automatically recognise when to use which view?

3.4 Conclusions

The problems above are just a few of the problems we have encountered in our attempt to fully automate the visualisation of algorithms and data structures based only on their source code. There are many other problems that are difficult or often impossible to solve either due to lack of knowledge concerning the algorithm's nature or because the semantics of the algorithm's operations cannot be deduced unambiguously. Implementing an undo/redo facility, defining meaningful input data, creating input validation functions, recognising conceptual input parameters, composing explanatory text, setting collapsible blocks, creating quizzes, etc. are just a few of them. Moreover, there is a strong coherence between the quality of a simulation and the automation's complexity. The more sophisticated a simulation should be, and the more requirements it is expected to meet, the more difficult is the automation. Nevertheless, just because a problem is difficult does not mean that it is insolvable. There is one class of algorithms that can be automatically simulated. These are the algorithms whose visualisation is a one-to-one mapping of the programme code and instructions to visual representations. In terms of the abstraction levels defined in Section 3.2, this is exactly the case when the programme level and the algorithm level of the simulation are the same. Apart from that, solving the problem of automation for arbitrary algorithms is equivalent to constructing artificial software that ultimately aims to emulate our own pedagogical and design abilities. In other words, it is equivalent to the problem of developing a machine which is able to understand an algorithm at the algorithm's level of abstraction, to think as a pedagogue, and to act as a programmer and a designer.

Chapter 4

An Approach to Semi-Automatic Generation of Visual Simulations

In this chapter, we present an approach to minimising the overall effort required for producing visual simulations. As it is not within the scope of this chapter to discuss the actual implementation details of the approach, these will be covered in the subsequent chapter.

We start by analysing the automation problems discussed in Chapter 3.3, and classify them into three groups. Based on this analysis, we introduce the key notion behind our approach and present its underlying concepts and mechanisms. In the second part of this chapter we go a step further and pay special attention to the three-dimensional passive animation of computational-intensive algorithms and algorithms for $\mathcal{NP}$-complete problems, as well as to the visualisation of parallel algorithms. In Section 4.3 we introduce an XML-based [133] approach for visualising the former class of algorithms. Section 4.4 introduces an approach for the easy development of visual simulations of parallel algorithms. The last section is dedicated to the visualisation of computer graphics algorithms. Here we will highlight some fundamental aspects of the development of visual simulations in this field.

4.1 Problem Analysis

Our analysis of the problems we encountered while attempting to visualise algorithms automatically revealed the following observations:

I. It turned out that in order to solve 15 of the 17 problems identified in the previous chapter, a visualising engine is required to be capable of understanding the abstractions, the semantics, and the overall logic of the algorithm as a human would do. In terms of the levels of abstraction introduced in Section 3.2, this means that the visualising engine is expected to understand the algorithm at the algorithm level rather than at the programme level, which is, indeed, a serious issue. These problems are 1-5, 7-9 and 11-17 (see Table 3).

Problem	Description
1	Identification and visualisation of fundamental abstract operations
2	Identification of primary and secondary data objects
3	Identification of access semantics
4	Focusing attention
5	Cloning data objects
6	Computation of geometrical coordinates and layout information
7	Displaying conceptual information
8	Extracting runtime information
9	Defining logical steps
10	Mapping data objects to visual objects
11	Defining meaningful input data
12	Creating input validation functions
13	Recognition of conceptual input parameters
14	Composing explanatory text
15	Setting collapsible blocks
16	Creating quizzes
17	Absence of data objects

Table 3: Problem overview

4.1. PROBLEM ANALYSIS

II. 12 of the 15 problems in the previous point (1-3, 5, 7-9, 11 and 13-16) relate to steps carried out by the pedagogue. It seems that the role of the pedagogue is difficult to automate.

III. Problems 2, 5, 8-10 and 15 can be comfortably eliminated if we incorporate simple additional information into the source code. Often, this information cannot be extracted from the source code, but can contribute to solving a large part of the problems.

IV. The automation of problems 11, 12, 14, 16 and 17 is extremely intricate and not recommended. It is unlikely that a machine can solve these problems better than a human could.

Based on these observations, and as a first step towards our approach, we classify the problems into three distinct clusters:

1. Cluster A includes all problems that can be easily solved by augmenting the source code of the algorithm with additional information regarding the nature of the included objects and operations. Augmenting the code is straightforward to accomplish, does not require much work and enables solving over half of the problems.

    Cluster A contains the following problems: Identification of primary and secondary data objects, cloning data objects, extracting runtime information, defining logical steps, mapping data objects to visual objects and defining collapsible blocks.

2. Cluster B comprises problems that can be automatically solved if the domain of the algorithms to be simulated is limited and well-known in advance. If our goal, for example, is to simulate a certain group of computer graphics algorithms or, say a group of sorting algorithms, then it would be possible to develop an automated domain-specific solution. It is, however, too difficult to automatically solve the problems for arbitrary algorithms.

The problems contained in cluster B are:

Identification and visualisation of fundamental abstract operations, identification of access semantics, focusing attention, computation of geometrical coordinates and layout information, displaying conceptual information, creating input validation functions and recognition of conceptual input parameters.

3. Cluster C consists of four intricate problems: 11, 14, 16 and 17. It is not recommended to solve these problems automatically, not only because they are too complex to be solved, but also because an automated solution would not always produce appealing results.

Hence, as we are concerned with simulating arbitrary algorithms, we will not attempt to solve these problems, and we will not consider the automation of visual simulation as our main goal. But rather, we seek to develop an approach to semi-automate the creation of visual simulations, and not to (semi)-automate the visualisation of simulations. In other words, we will not semi-automate the simulation process itself, but the process of creating simulations (see this chapter's title).

This has lead us to develop an approach that circumvents all 'B-problems' and, at the same time, solves the 'A-problems' simply by using a code augmentation technique. In the following section we introduce this approach.

4.2 Semi-Automated Approach

Our approach is a combination of full automation, semi-automation and manual intervention. The approach is geared towards eliminating the problems of the first cluster, getting around the problems of the second and manually solving the problems of the third one. It is based on the idea of transforming the algorithm's code into simulation code by using three concepts: visual objects, source code augmentation and reusable parameterised components. The resulting simulation code

4.2. SEMI-AUTOMATED APPROACH

encloses the visual instructions that constitute the entire visualisation or at least a substantial part of it. Some of the simulation's components can be constructed fully automatically based on the information included in the source code after augmentation. Others are generated semi-automatically with the aid of meta-data and reusable parameterised components. The rest, which can neither be created automatically nor semi-automatically, is constructed manually. Thus, the approach requires some degree of manual intervention into the algorithm's source code.

We now introduce the three aforementioned concepts.

4.2.1 Visual objects

A visual object is a graphical representation of a data object. It exhibits a set of visual operations that mirror its current state and allow for the modification of its data, appearance and location. Our approach involves replacing all key data objects of the algorithm by visual objects, and replacing any interesting data operation by its corresponding visual one. Recall from Section 2.7.1 that each algorithm operates on a set of data objects (variables, arrays, graphs, trees, etc.). Depicting these objects and their operations constitutes a large part of the visualisation. Thus, the replacement process will help generate a large fragment of the simulation code. It is important to note at this point that the simulation does not need to be concerned about how visual objects work. It handles them as black boxes that provide interfaces representing the visual operations that they can perform on themselves, or to communicate with each other (bridges). Listing B.5 shows the code of a visual array implemented as a visual object.

By using the concept of visual objects, we reduce the effort required for implementing the visualisation part of each individual simulation, to the work needed to find and replace the data objects and operations by their corresponding visual ones[1]. To automate this process, we need a mechanism that helps us easily identify

---
[1] Remember that implementing the graphics portion of the visualisation is the most laborious part of the entire process.

these objects in the algorithm's code. The mechanism we use for this purpose is code augmentation.

4.2.2 Code augmentation

Code augmentation is a technique that refers to the incorporation of meta-data and annotations into the algorithm's source code. The purpose of the augmentation is to enrich the source code with supplementary information regarding its artefacts.

Given the source code of an algorithm in a high-level programming language, we annotate the code to provide the code generator (see below) with the ability to identify crucial elements and construct parts of the simulation. Among others, we mark the following elements:

1. Key data objects and their abstract operations

2. Data objects that need to be cloned

3. Locations of the control points

4. Start and end of logical steps

5. Collapsible blocks

6. Operations that affect the runtime analysis of the algorithm

7. Narratives

8. Links to documentations or tutorials

A code generator processes the augmented source code and transforms it into simulation code. This is primarily achieved by replacing the marked data objects and operations by their visual matches. In addition, it replaces some meta-data directives by code instructions. These instructions enable the simulation to bind

4.2. SEMI-AUTOMATED APPROACH

and use parameterised graphical components and provide them with the accurate data.

When applying the meta-data, we automatically eliminate all the problems of cluster A and enable the code generator to bind the following components:

Runtime information display, control points, collapsible blocks, documentation display, narrative display, and graphical view. All these components except the last one are referred to as reusable parameterised components.

Listing B.1 shows a simplified example of an augmented source code excerpt of binary search trees.

4.2.3 Reusable parameterised components

Reusable parameterised components are graphical or non-graphical components that can be readily adjusted to be used by any simulation. A good example of a reusable component is the source code listing display (see Figure 4). It obtains, as a parameter, several listings of the source code of the algorithm that a simulation wishes to display. The listings can be given in a pseudo code notation and/or various notations of programming languages, in which case, each will be displayed in a separate tab. The code listing display uses an integrated non-graphical component called syntax colourer. The syntax colourer is a reusable parameterised component that receives two parameters: a source code listing and a flag indicating the programming language in which the code is written. The output of the syntax colourer is a specification of how the code listing display should colour the syntax of the given code. It is obvious that we use meta-data to specify the locations of the files containing the various source code forms.

A code scanner is another example of a reusable component. Listing B.2 shows the source code of a Python scanner implemented in Java.

Figure 12 shows arrangements of the components in groups indicating how each component is created according to our approach.

74 CHAPTER 4. SEMI-AUTOMATIC APPROACH

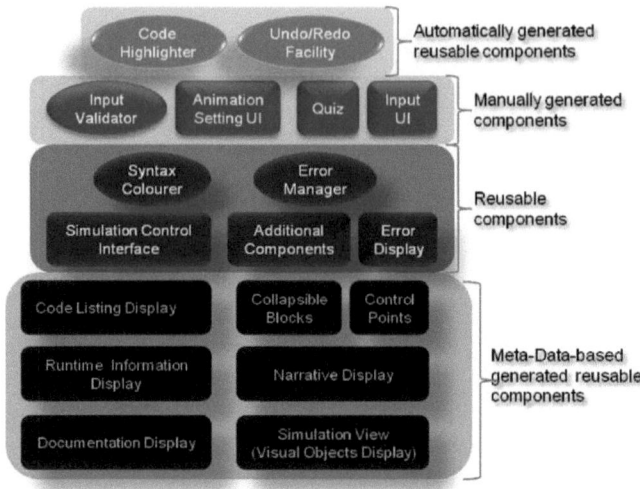

Figure 12: Grouping the simulation components based on their creation method

Thus, according to our approach the parts of a simulation are constructed in three ways:

- Using special meta-data notation:

  The meta-data marks the data objects and operations, and specifies which components a simulation needs and which input these components should be fed with. A code generator fetches the components from a library and binds them in the simulation code.

- Automatically:

  The code generator creates the component fully automatically based on the source code of the algorithm. The only two components that can be created in this way are the code listing highlighter and the undo/redo manager; both of which will be covered in Section 5.4 and 5.5, respectively.

- Manually:

4.2. SEMI-AUTOMATED APPROACH

In many circumstances the code generator will not be able to create simulations tailored for each purpose. Some components of the simulation have to be coded manually. This applies particularly to the interesting data input, the user interfaces for input and settings parameters, and the quiz component. Additionally, the developer might wish to extend the default implementation of some components, or to enhance or complete some code parts.

Figure 13 shows an illustration of the approach.

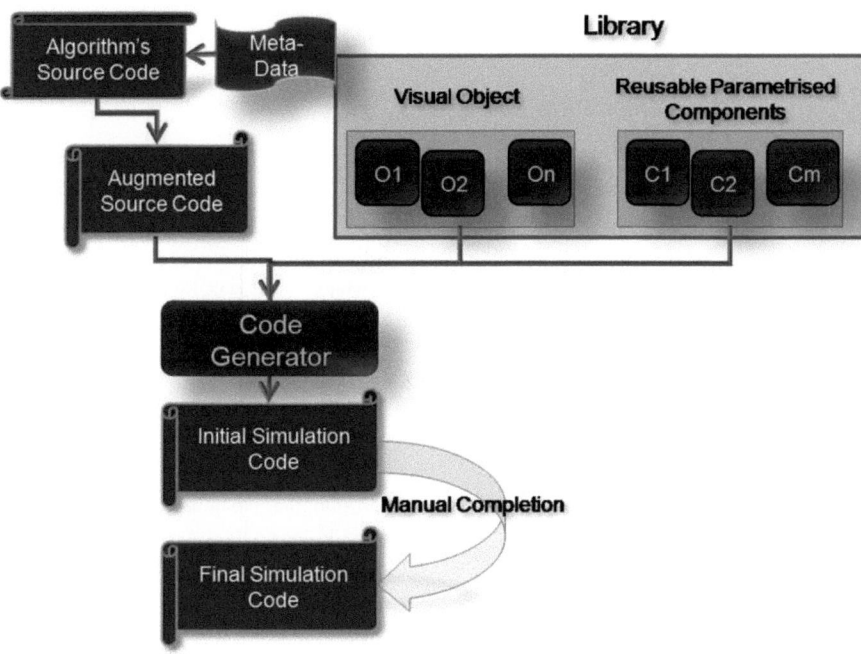

Figure 13: Semi-automatic approach for creating visual simulations

4.3 Animation of Computation-Intensive Algorithms and Algorithms for $\mathcal{NP}$-Complete Problems

The visual simulation approach is applicable to algorithms with reasonable runtime. It is, however, completely inappropriate for computation-intensive algorithms [56, 128]. Due to their potentially enormous execution time, computation-intensive algorithms and algorithms for $\mathcal{NP}$-complete problems (hereafter referred to as ANPP), cannot be simulated in real time for arbitrary input length. Animation authors are here often forced to follow the passive animation approach, even though this form of visualisation is not considered notably effective [13].

There are two methods for designing passive 3D animations of algorithms:

- Using a 3D high-level programming language
- Using a 3D animation language

Both approaches have advantages and drawbacks that will be covered in the evaluation Section 6.3.

In our work, we follow the second approach. Thus, in order to broaden the scope of visualisable algorithms, we have developed the first 3D algorithm animation standard (an algorithm animation language) and an animation engine (an animation player) which have enabled us to design and play passive animations of ANPP. The work presented in this section covers the essential aspects of the language and draws on the following two publications: [12], [60].

4.3.1 An algorithm animation language for 3D algorithms

Although the language we are introducing in this subsection can be used to animate arbitrary 3D algorithms, it is primarily intended to be used for designing animations of ANPP. It is our belief that non-computational-intensive algorithms should be simulated using a high-level graphics API rather than being animated passively.

4.3. ANIMATION OF COMPUTATION-INTENSIVE ALGORITHMS AND ALGORITHMS FOR $\mathcal{NP}$-COMPLETE PROBLEMS

Prior to developing a new standard or a language, a set of requirements should be specified:

One of the key requirements for a flexible and powerful animation language is its ability to support modelling and utilisation of data structures and their associated operations. This means that complex data structures (trees, graphs, multi-dimensional arrays, etc.) should be fully supported or at least easy to construct. Furthermore, the language should be easy to learn. Authors with none or only sparse programming skills, should be given the opportunity to create animations without additional effort. For the syntax of the language, a platform-independent and portable format should be used which not only supports the manual, but also the tool-based animation creation (creation of scripts)[2]. Likewise, it should be possible to readily parse, interpret and exchange scripts and convert them into scripts specified in other animation languages. Since the widespread XML standard [133] supports the last requirement, it forms the basis of the syntax of our new language.

An already existing XML standard, which supports the creation of general animations, is the well known X3D standard [131]. X3D is an XML-based 3D description language for interactive 3D content, which could also be used for the animation of algorithms and data structures. Before we started developing a new standard, we took the application of X3D into consideration. An extensive analysis, however, has revealed its unsuitability as an algorithm animation standard for many reasons:

- X3D is too powerful. In order to be applicable, the entire scheme must be first learned. This contradicts our demand for an easy-to-learn language.

- In order to use complex data structures, a huge number of graphic primitives must be instantiated and carefully combined to constitute the desired data structures.

- Algorithm-animation-specific concepts, like displaying source code listings,

---

[2]The term "script" is used to denote the file that includes a specification of an algorithm animation written in a certain animation language.

code-highlighting, syntax-colouring, quizzes, narratives, etc. must be coded manually.

- The embedding of an existent X3D interpreter into an existing algorithm animation system can be very complicated. A complete reprogramming of an X3D interpreter would be too complex, not only due to the implementation of an undo/redo functionality, but also due to the efforts needed to embed it into an existing system.

Anslow et al. who recently used X3D to develop web-based animations reported more problems [7]. For all these reasons we decided to develop a new XML standard which we named **xml3DVis**. A brief introduction of xml3DVis' most important components is given in the following subsection. Interested readers are encouraged to read more about the standard in the cited works.

Conceptual structure

An xml3DVis animation is specified in an xml3DVis script which is a file with the extension "x3v" that can include a collection of the following segments:

```
<xml3DVis>
    <metadata>          ... </metadata>
    <boundings>         ... </boundings>
    <objects>           ... </objects>
    <scene>             ... </scene>
    <sounds>            ... </sounds>
    <operations>        ... </operations>
    <codeFormatters>    ... </codeFormatters>
    <code>              ... </code>
    <keyframes>         ... </keyframes>
    <documentation>     ... </documentation>
</xml3DVis>
```

The segment "MetaData" can be used not only to store information regarding the data file, such as author, version, etc., but also general information concerning the animation parameters and speed. Boundings-elements are elements for the

4.3. ANIMATION OF COMPUTATION-INTENSIVE ALGORITHMS AND ALGORITHMS FOR $\mathcal{NP}$-COMPLETE PROBLEMS

definition of the visibility scope of objects and their activation region. The segment 'Objects' can be used to globally define objects that will be bound later on during the animation. Features for modifying the appearance of graphical objects (e.g., colour, texture, illumination parameters, etc.) can be defined with the aid of Appearance-elements. xml3DVis supports 21 graphic primitives and geometrical structures for composing more complex objects or for the definition of complex data structures if needed. Together with the support of conventional data structures (such as multidimensional arrays, trees, graphs, etc.) xml3DVis fulfils one of the essential requirements we specified earlier. Operations supported by xml3DVis can be divided into the following three categories:

- Animation operations which can be performed on graphic primitives.

- Event-dependent operations which can be executed at the beginning or at the end of a keyframe [127] whenever a certain event occurs, such as *playSound*, *showQuiz*, *setAppearance*, *setText*, etc.

- Data structure operations for the manipulation of data structures, e.g., *add*, *remove*, *search*, etc.

xml3DVis also supports the display of test assignments in the form of single- or multiple choice questions (quiz), as well as narrative texts.

The segment 'Code' can be used to define code listings. The language also provides mechanisms for highlighting code lines during the animation. xml3DVis provides syntax colouring support for pseudo code listings as well as for codes written in various notations.

An animation specified in xml3DVis includes a sequence of time segments called keyframes. A keyframe encompass specifications of all visual objects and operations that will be rendered later in a visual frame. When the xml3DVis animation player plays an animation, it maps each of its keyframes to a visual frame. This results in a film composed of a sequence of visual frames that build the entire animation.

80 CHAPTER 4. SEMI-AUTOMATIC APPROACH

For a better understanding of the animated algorithm or data structure, xml3DVis offers the animation author the possibility to display learning materials and documentations.

With the support of the aforementioned features, xml3DVis allows the animation of a wide range of algorithms and data structures. However, we will show in Subsection 6.3 that there are also algorithms which stretch every algorithm animation language to its limits.

Figure 14 shows the conceptual structure of xml3DVis.

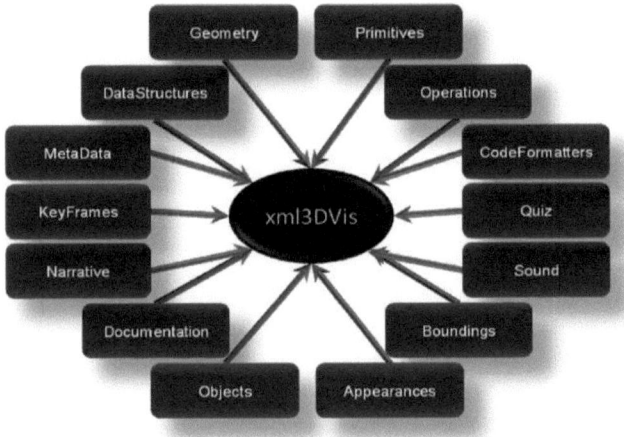

Figure 14: Conceptual structure of xml3DVis

In addition to the language, we have implemented a visualisation engine consisting of an interpreter, a mapper and an animation player. The interpreter includes an XML parser that parses xml3DVis files and checks them for validity and consistency. The mapper maps xml3DVis elements to a data model. The animation player is responsible for analysing the data model, transforming it into 3D graphic primitives and animated operations.

4.3. ANIMATION OF COMPUTATION-INTENSIVE ALGORITHMS AND ALGORITHMS FOR $\mathcal{NP}$-COMPLETE PROBLEMS

4.3.2 Animating the TSP with xml3DVis

To demonstrate the strength of xml3DVis, we present a visualisation of the travelling-salesman problem (TSP) [45] for eight vertices. According to our classification in Section 2.1, the algorithm of the TSP is an augmented two-dimensional algorithm. We chose this problem for the following three reasons:

- To demonstrate the application of xml3DVis on a real world example.
- To show how complex the creation of animations can become.
- To give an impression of how powerful xml3DVis is.

The TSP is $\mathcal{NP}$-complete [45, 128, 81], and thus not solvable by any algorithm in polynomial time. All known algorithms for solving this problem require exponential runtime.

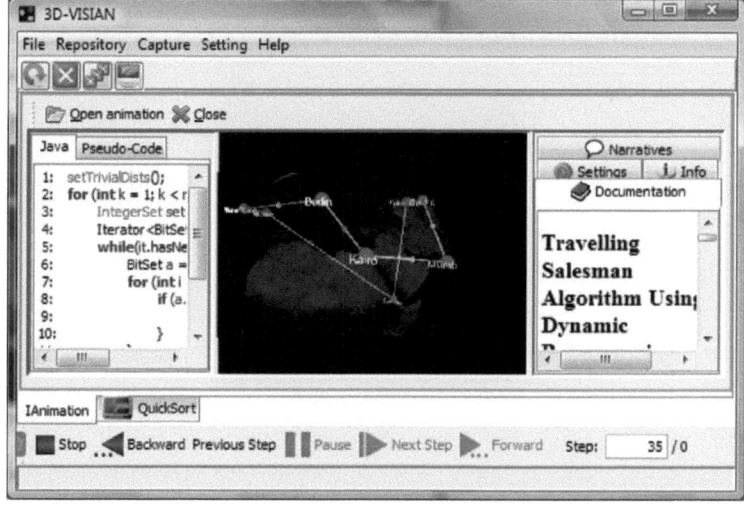

Figure 15: Animation of the TSP in 3D-Visian

Even using a small number of vertices, a non-visual simulation of this problem reaches enormous execution time. Näher [81] has shown that for eight vertices only a few minutes are needed to compute the optimal route when using the brute-force method, i.e., computing all possible paths, while for 16 vertices approximately 20 years are needed. It is impossible to get the complexity problem completely under control even by using an alternative design paradigm. A different approach for 16 vertices using dynamic programming [45] requires a running time of a couple of hours. A simulation for eight vertices requires 1145 steps (nine vertices require 5623 steps). In order to avoid the gigantic execution time, a static animation has been used to visualise the problem. All intermediate steps have been computed in advance, several steps have been combined during the animation into a representative one. Thus the actual computation time has been reasonably reduced. As the computation of the intermediate steps could not be done manually, we created a separate programme to compute them. Another programme was needed to generate the xml3DVis file of the whole animation. Obviously, in the case of eight vertices it is also possible to simulate the algorithm instead of using a static animation. However, from a didactical point of view, it neither makes sense to see the same steps again and again, nor is it acceptable to wait until the computation of the next interesting step has been completed. For this reason, it seems to be more reasonable to select some pedagogically valuable steps, than showing every single one. Omitting all the non-interesting steps has not only minimised the execution time of the animation and improved its performance, but has also increased the learning effect.

An evaluation of this approach will be conducted in Section 6.3. Figure 16 shows all possible connections between the eight vertices on the left side and the optimal route on the right side.

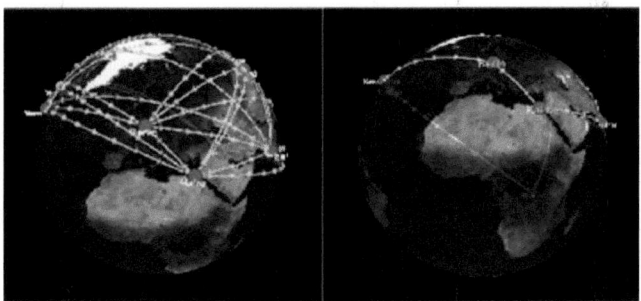

Figure 16: Travelling-salesman problem on a textured sphere created in xml3DVis

4.4 Visual Simulation of Parallel Algorithms

Parallel and distributed algorithms constitute an advanced topic in theoretical and practical computer science that has gained much interest recently. It is generally known that studying and teaching the fundamentals of parallel algorithm's concepts present a constant challenge to both learners and educators. Due to the additional abstract concepts applied in the implementation of parallel algorithms, designing visualisations of parallel algorithms is far more arduous than visualising sequential ones (single process). At the same time, the pedagogical gain of parallel algorithm visualisations is much higher than that of sequential algorithms.

In this section we introduce a new approach to minimising the effort needed to create effective visual simulations of parallel algorithms. The work presented in this section is greatly influenced by a joint research done together with Maksim Mosgowoi [80]. Given there is a chance that some readers will not be familiar with parallel algorithms, we have provided a brief introduction about the topic. This introduction is necessary to understand this section and is based on [102]. It is by no means comprehensive and should not be assumed as a substitution for the cited literature.

4.4.1 Parallel algorithms

A parallel algorithm is an algorithm which can be simultaneously executed by several different processes[3]. Each process handles a part of the input data and communicates with the other processes to compute the final result in a more efficient way [102, 67, 19, 93]. In order for the processes to communicate with each other, they use a so-called communication pattern. A communication pattern describes the structure employed to distribute the information among the processes efficiently. Formally, a communication pattern is an undirected graph, whose nodes each correspond to a process. Each graph edge represents a connection between two communicating processes. The most frequently used communication patterns are binary trees, meshes, hypercubes and butterfly networks [102]. Apart from communication patterns, parallel algorithms also differ from sequential algorithms in the way in which the data is distributed among the processes. To send and receive data, processes use special operations called communication routines. A widely used library containing a number of communication routines is the MPI [89]. This interface comprises primitive and collective communication routines. Primitive communication routines consist of simple send and receive operations, which can be applied in several modes (e.g. buffered, synchronous, immediate, etc.) between two particular processes. Collective communication routines are far more complicated, as they make powerful communications possible, involving many (or even all) processes at once. The most used collective communication routines are: *Broadcast, Scatter, Gather, Reduce, Scan, AllGather, AllToAll* and *AllReduce* (see [102] for more details).

Another two aspects, which parallel algorithms (but not sequential ones) need to be concerned with, are partitioning and mapping. Prior to a computation step, the

---

[3] In the literature two models of parallel computing are often distinguished: multi-computers using distributed memory where each computer has only access to its own separate memory; and multiprocessors with one single shared memory [101]. As this distinction bears no impact on the visualisation, we have not taken this differentiation into account throughout this section and assume that input data will be in the end processed by processes, regardless of the underlying model.

4.4. VISUAL SIMULATION OF PARALLEL ALGORITHMS

processes need to obtain their respective parts of input data. This step is separated into two phases: the partitioning and the mapping phase. The former refers to the decomposition of data into fragments and assigning the fragments to primitive tasks (parts of the computations). The latter denotes the process of combining primitive tasks into larger ones and assigning them to corresponding processes. There are several decomposition methods designed to support various data structures. When it comes to matrix-based algorithms there are four major decomposition methods: row-wise, column-wise, diagonal, and checkerboard decomposition [102].

4.4.2 Visualisation aspects of parallel algorithms

The visualisation of parallel algorithms poses stronger demands than does the visualisation of sequential algorithms. In addition to the large number of requirements for visual simulations of sequential algorithms (see Section 2), there are four further essential requirements a visualisation of a parallel algorithm is expected to fulfil:

- Synchronisation:

  In a real visual simulation of a parallel algorithm, the processes are normally executed using threads. As the goal of a visualisation is not just to show the results of the executing tasks, but to illustrate how these results gradually evolve in a certain order, we demand a synchronisation of the executing threads. The purpose of the synchronisation is to yield a controlled visualisation of the computation rather than to obtain a random one.

- Providing an appropriate representation of the communication pattern.

- Providing an appropriate visualisation of the data decomposition and mapping.

- Providing an appropriate visualisation of the primitive and collective communication routines.

4.4.3 Clustering approach

Our approach to reducing the effort required to design visual simulations for parallel algorithms is based on analysing a reasonable number of parallel algorithms and clustering them in respect to the effort required for the visualisation. All members of a cluster are, from a visualisation perspective, very similar and can be visualised in the same manner. Providing a visualisation of just any one, this visualisation can be adopted to derive new ones for all other members. Thus, the effort required to visualise the entire cluster is reduced to the work needed to implement one algorithm and adapting the implementation so that it fits to each of the remaining algorithms.

Although we considered all the following classes of algorithms, we examined the ones listed below bold.

- Matrix-Multiplication: (**Matrix Vector Algorithm, Fox Algorithm, Cannon Algorithm**, DNS Algorithm)

- Systems of Linear Equations: (**Back Substitution, Gaussian Elimination**, Iterative Methods, Finite Difference Methods)

- Discrete Fourier Transformation: (**FFT**, Binary Exchange Algorithm, Transpose Algorithm)

- Sorting with Divide-&-Conquer: (**Parallel Quicksort, Hyperquicksort, Sample Sort**, Parallel Merge Sort)

- Dynamic Programming: (**Warshall Algorithm, Floyd Algorithm**, Global Pairwise Alignment, RNA Secondary Structure Prediction)

- Miscellaneous: (**Prefix Evaluation Problem, Odd-Even Transposition Sort, Shearsort**)

We chose these algorithms for the following reasons:

4.4. VISUAL SIMULATION OF PARALLEL ALGORITHMS

- The selected algorithms of the category "Sorting with Divide-&-Conquer" use sophisticated communication routines, such as BCast, Gather and Scan. This allows for a visual illustration of these forms of communication.

- The algorithms Fox, Cannon, Warshall, Floyd, Back Substitution, and Gaussian Elimination cover several aspects of data decomposition and mapping.

- The Matrix-Vector Algorithm combines sophisticated communication routines with elaborate decomposition and mapping.

- The Prefix Evaluation Problem on the one hand, and the Odd-Even Transposition Sort and Shearsort on the other, use a binary tree and a mesh as communication patterns, respectively.

Thus, the selection allows for a demonstration of many visualisation aspects of parallel algorithms.

Our investigation focuses on the visualisation aspects of the algorithms. We examined how the visualisation of the data structures, the data decomposition and mapping, the communication patterns and the communication routines can affect the visualisation complexity.

All algorithms of the categories Matrix-Multiplication, Linear Systems and Dynamic Programming use matrices as data structures. Thus, row-wise, column-wise and checkerboard decomposition are typical decomposition methods that can be used for all these algorithms except the Back Substitution algorithm, which uses diagonal decomposition. Similarly, the algorithms of the categories Sorting with Divide-&-Conquer, and Miscellaneous use arrays. These algorithms divide the array into blocks (subarrays) and distribute these subarrays among the processes.

As for communication routines, the choice of an appropriate communication routine for an algorithm strongly depends upon its design. We could not find any link between the utilised communication routine on the one hand and the used data or the type of the problem on the other. Both matrix-based and array-based algorithms, e.g., use primitive and collective communication routines.

One can also observe that there is no connection between the data structures used and the communication routines. Algorithms that use matrices arrays apply the same communication routines.

The communication pattern employed depends in many cases on the underlying data structure and the applied data decomposition method. A matrix-based algorithm uses row-wise or column-wise decomposition and one-dimensional mesh as communication pattern. If the data in the matrix is partitioned using checkerboard decomposition, the utilised communication pattern is a two-dimensional mesh. This was noticed, e.g., in the categories Matrix-Multiplication and Sorting with Divide-&-Conquer. The communication pattern of Fourier Transformation, Hyperquicksort and the Prefix Evaluation Problem, however, are determined independently of the data structures. These algorithms use a butterfly network, hypercube and binary tree, respectively.

Examining the algorithms from a visualisation perspective has revealed the following:

- The visualisation complexity highly depends upon the data structure rather than the communication pattern, or the communication routines.

- As the data decomposition is dependent upon the data structure, its visualisation is dependent, accordingly, on the visualisation of the data structure.

- Since any communication pattern can be modelled as a graph and because the visualisation of any graph does not present a huge challenge, communication patterns do not considerably affect the visualisation complexity.

- The visualisation of the communication routines can be basically accomplished by drawing the path which the data travels towards its destination processes. Hence, the visualisation of the communication routines does not considerably affect the overall complexity of the visualisation.

4.4. VISUAL SIMULATION OF PARALLEL ALGORITHMS

Based on these observations, four clusters were constructed (see Table 4).

Cluster	Algorithm(s)
Matrix-Algorithms	Matrix-Vector Multiplication, Fox Algorithm, Canon Algorithm, Back Substitution, Gaussian Elimination, Warshall Algorithm, Floyd Algorithm
Array-Algorithms	Parallel Quicksort, Hyperquicksort, Samplesort, Odd-Even Transposition Sort, Shearsort
Miscellaneous1	Prefix Evaluation Problem
Miscellaneous2	Fast Fourier Transform

Table 4: Clustering of the investigated algorithms

The Matrix-Algorithms cluster encompasses algorithms that use a matrix as a data structure.

The second cluster includes algorithms which operate on arrays. These algorithms use one-dimensional meshes and block decomposition.

The last two clusters contain one algorithm each. None of these analysed algorithms can be assigned to any of the first clusters. They apply specific data structures that are not used by any of the remaining algorithms.

By using this clustering strategy, we have successfully created effective visualisations of the algorithms presented in this section with little effort. The clustering of similar algorithms has proven to greatly facilitate the visualisation process. When we compare how much effort usually needed to visualise each algorithm separately to the effort required to implement our approach, one can see that our method has significantly reduced the work needed to implement this rather complex group of algorithms. This approach is not restricted to a particular class of parallel algorithms, but can be applied to arbitrary classes as well.

4.5 Simulation of Computer Graphics Algorithms

Computer graphics algorithms pose more visualisation difficulties than conventional algorithms do. Most computer graphics algorithms are inherently individual, have little in common and operate on distinct geometrical objects using various approaches and techniques. Raster graphics algorithms for drawing 2D primitives, e.g., operate on 2D pixel grids and draw their primitives by setting individual pixels of the grid. 2D clipping algorithms work also in a 2D plane, even though they operate on points, lines and polygons, and compute intersections by solving linear equation systems. Volume ray tracing algorithms operate on three-dimensional spatial data to compute coloured 2D projections of it. Ray tracing is not the only technique employed for volume rendering. Other techniques such as marching cubes and rendering voxels in binary partitioned space are also for the same purpose; however, they follow completely different approaches. We use the ray tracing technique not only for volume rendering, but also for visible surface determination, and in illumination and shading in combination with shading models. In addition to ray tracers, the Z-Buffer and the painter's algorithm are further algorithms for hidden surface removal in 3D and have only two things in common: the goal and the geometrical object they work on. Implementing a radiosity simulation to illuminate a scene requires the use of a completely different approach than implementing the same simulation for the same scene using ray tracing.

From the recent discussion one can infer that, due to the fact that computer graphics algorithms are very different, they are harder to visualise, compared to conventional algorithms, which have a lot in common. Even graphics algorithms that solve the same problem could quickly stretch our proposed approach to its limits (see the evaluation of the approach in Section 6.2).

Chapter 5

Implementation

This chapter focuses on the implementation aspects of the semi-automatic approach as well as the concepts introduced in the previous chapter. In particular, we will introduce an environment for the development of arbitrary 3D algorithm visualisations. This environment is composed from the following units:

- A code generator for the semi-automatic creation of simulations, as proposed in the previous chapter.

- An algorithm visualisation 3D programming interface (VPI). This VPI is a 3D library comprising a large collection of auxiliary components and serves as a rich programming interface for the development of algorithm visualisations.

- A modern algorithm visualisation system that we have designed and implemented to serve as an execution platform for arbitrary passive animations and visual simulations.

After briefly introducing the technologies used in the development, we describe the specification techniques we have employed to implement the code augmentation concept. Next, we give an insight into the interior of the code generator and highlight its key components. Section 5.4 introduces a facility for the automatic highlighting of code listings. Section 5.5 presents an extension of the Java API that we have developed for the construction of undoable 3D applications in general, and undoable algorithm visualisations in particular. We conclude this chapter by proposing an architecture for the design and implementation of algorithm visualisation systems. As an application of this proposal, we present 3D-Visian — our algorithm visualisation system/platform.

5.1 Implementation Technologies

The primary steps towards implementing an algorithm visualisation environment entail deciding on appropriate implementation techniques and technologies. In our development we primarily employ two implementation technologies (Java and Java 3D) and one technique (AST).

So far our experiences have shown, Java [120] and Java 3D [9, 29] are outstanding technologies for implementing algorithm visualisations and visualisation systems. This is due to their platform independence and web compatibility. In particular, Java 3D has become one of the most popular 3D APIs, which in recent times has been widely used to develop both web-based and standalone 3D applications. Introducing Java and Java 3D in depth is not within the scope of this work. In order to understand some of the subsequent sections, the reader should have familiarity with Java 3D's basic terminology and concepts. Therefore we have prepared a brief introduction to the fundamentals of Java 3D and included it in Appendix C.1. This introduction, however, is in no way comprehensive. For detailed literature, the reader is advised to consult the Java 3D specification or one of the following resources: [108, 119, 68].

An AST [3] is an abstraction for parsing, processing and modifying the source code of a programme. As it forms a key component of the code generator, it will be dealt with in the following subsection more closely.

5.1. IMPLEMENTATION TECHNOLOGIES

5.1.1 Abstract Syntax Tree (AST)

In general, an Abstract Syntax Tree is a tree representation of the structure and the content of a source code written in a certain programming language. An AST implementation is usually used to parse, process, modify and perform structural and semantic analyses of programme code. In particular, we use an AST to parse the source code of an algorithm written in Java and map it to a tree model. Each node in the resulting tree corresponds to a Java element (a field declaration, an assignment, a method, a loop, etc.). The AST offers a wealth of methods and properties that can be used to access and modify these nodes. Any modification to the tree model is transmitted to its underlying Java code (see Figure 17). The code generator uses an AST as a facility to transform the algorithm's source code into simulation code.

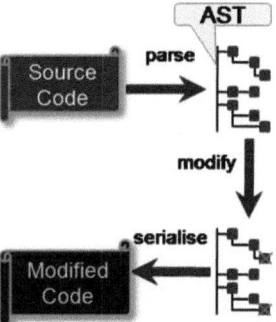

Figure 17: Illustration of an Abstract Syntax Tree

To see an example of an AST, refer to the class "OwnerSetter" in Listing B.4.

5.2 Code Augmentation Techniques

The purpose of code augmentation is to annotate the algorithm's source code with meta information that assists the code generator understand the semantics of particular elements in the code to automatically generate parts of the simulation code. We use two techniques to augment the source code without violating the syntax of the language:

- Ordinary Java comments (implementation comments), and

- Java annotations

The term "ordinary" is used to distinguish between the implementation comments and the documentation comments (Doc comments) used in Java. The latter describe the specification of the code from an implementation-free perspective, to be read by developers who might not necessarily have the source code at hand[1].

The implementation comments we used to augment the code are called Visian comments. To be distinguishable from other comments, Visian multiple line comments start with /*~ and end with */. A line comment start with // .

Java annotations [5] are meta-data about Java programme units. Java allows programmers to define their own annotation types and to use them at different places in their code. Java, additionally, provides a set of built-in annotations which are frequently used in programming; among these are *@Deprecated* and *@Override*. The *@Override* annotation informs the compiler that the annotated element is meant to override an element declared in a superclass. The *@Deprecated* annotation indicates that the marked element is deprecated and should no longer be used. As can be seen, each annotation starts with an @-sign.

Both methods (using comments and using annotations) have advantages and disadvantages. The advantage of using annotations over using comments is that Java

---

[1]To learn more about the difference between the two types of comments, visit the following site [28].

provides a built-in annotation processor, which can readily be used to process annotations at compile and runtime. However, unlike Java comments, annotations have the restriction that they can only be used to annotate classes, methods, variables, parameters and packages. Comments, on the other hand, can be placed nearly everywhere in the source code. However, using comments to incorporate meta-data in a code has two drawbacks:

- It requires us to define a special syntax for the tags that will be included in the comments (see Listing B.1 as an example for an augmented code snippet).

- It imposes the implementation of a processor with which the tags can be processed and made accessible for the code generator.

Among others, we use annotations as markers to denote, the key data objects and their abstract operations which will be visualised, the data objects that need to be cloned, and the methods whose lines should be highlighted at execution time.

Java comments are used for denoting the following items and many others: locations of control points, beginnings and endings of logical steps, collapsible blocks, narratives, and runtime information.

Code listing B.1 shows an augmented code of the *delete* operation of binary search trees. Code listing B.4 shows the implementation of the Visian comment parser class. The class uses an AST to parse and process the Visian comments included in an augmented code.

5.3 Code Generator

The code generator is the facility used to parse the augmented version of the algorithm's source code into an abstract syntax tree. To exploit the useful services of some Eclipse [50] tools, the code generator has been implemented as an Eclipse plug-in [27]. Instead of discussing all details of the code generator, we will present its essential components and briefly highlight their functions:

96   CHAPTER 5.   IMPLEMENTATION

The code generator is instrumented with the following tools:

- Preprocessor

- Code listing mapper

- Component generator

The conceptual structure of the code generator is illustrated in Figure 18.

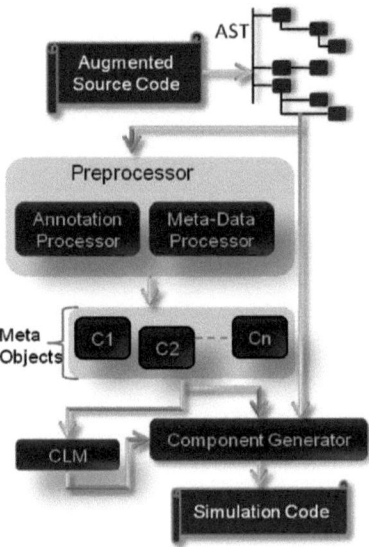

Figure 18: Structure of the code generator

The **preprocessor** is a component composed of two units: a **meta-data processor** and an **annotation processor**. The former is responsible for processing the meta-data included in the Visian comments and mapping it to internal data objects called 'meta objects'. The meta objects constitute the input for the component generator. With their aid, the code generator will be able to create instances of the components specified in the meta-data, supply them with the appropriate parameters, and enclose them in the simulation context. The annotation processor has the same functionality, however, it generates the meta objects based on the provided annotations.

The **code listing mapper** (CLM) is the code generator's component which creates a mapping of the algorithm's source code to the algorithm's code listing. This mapping is later passed to the component generator and used to create the code highlighter (see Section 5.4).

As the name indicates, the **component generator** is the facility of the code generator which is responsible for creating instances of simulation components and visual objects, and binding them in the simulation code.

5.4 Automatic Code Highlighting

The **code highlighter** is the facility that ties the simulation core to the code listing display. Whenever a set of instructions in the simulation code is executed, the simulation requests the highlighter to highlight the corresponding code lines in the code listing display. To do so, the simulation passes the line numbers as a parameter to the code highlighter. The highlighter maintains a table that includes mappings of the simulation instructions to the source code lines. Each set of code instructions is mapped there to a set of lines in the display. Creating this mapping by hand is tedious, and fortunately unnecessary. We have developed a mechanism that generates this mapping automatically based on the source code of the algorithm. What follows is an illustration of this mechanism.

5.4.1 Source code-based automatic highlighting

As previously mentioned, the **Code Listing Mapper** (CLM) is the component of the code generator which is responsible for generating the mapping passed to the highlighter. After the preprocessing of the meta-data, the CLM is the first component that the code generator sets into action. The first task that the CLM performs is to extract a legible copy of the algorithm's code. To do so, the CLM creates a copy of the source code and cleans it by removing all meta-data and unnecessary documentation comments. The resulting text is the listing that will appear later in the code display. No meta-data or annotations appear anymore. While cleaning the source code, the CLM uses a table to note the numbers of the lines that have been removed. With the aid of this table, it can later recognise which code instructions in the original code correspond to which code lines in the copy. Suppose, for example, that the line number of a code instruction that stands in the original source code at line n needs to be mapped to line number m in the source code copy. Suppose further, that k unnecessary code lines following line n have been removed, and are therefore not present in the copy. With the help of the table, the CLM will be able to recognise that line n in the original code should be mapped to line $n - k = m$ in the copy. This sounds obvious, which is true if we do line-wise mapping. This would be, however, inefficient. Fortunately it is unnecessary. That is because, if we assume that a code line contains one single instruction; whenever this instruction has been finally executed, the code generator will indicate this by highlighting the corresponding line in the code listing display. This means that the simulation code must include a call to the code highlighter after each instruction.

Hence, a simulation of an algorithm with 50 code lines would include 50 highlight calls. This would slow down the performance of the simulation and make its code look bulky. Instead, the CLM maps the original code to the copy set-wise, and not line-wise. That is, it collects a set of consecutive code lines in the original code and maps them to their correspondences in the copy. The question is: Which strategies does the CLM apply to perform this mapping? This is a question that we will answer in the following subsection.

5.4.2 Set-wise code line mapping

To create a set-wise code line mapping we use the AST of the code generator. To simplify the discussion, we will assume that the code instructions we seek to map are enclosed in a method (a routine or a procedure).

The CLM distinguishes between three classes of code statements: jump statements, block statements and standard statements. A **jump statement** is a statement that can cause the execution flow of a method to be interrupted and/or to be continued at a code line outside the method. In Java, a jump statement can be a method invocation statement, a *return*, a *break*, an *assert*, a *throw* or a *continue* statement. The latter is the only statement that causes the execution of a method to be interrupted and continued at a line inside the method. A **block statement** is any statement that has a body enclosed by curly brackets. In Java, this can be a *while*, a *for*, or a *do* loop, an *if*, a *switch*, a *try*, or a *synchronized* statement. A **standard statement** denotes any other statement, such as an assignment, a field declaration, a cast statement, etc. A code segment has a start and an end statement. An end statement can either be a jump or a block statement or it can be the end of a method or a block. A start statement can be the start of a method or the first statement following an end statement. We now illustrate how the CLM acts using the code example in listing 5.1.

The left listing shows the source code of the *successor* and *minimum* methods used by a binary search tree. For convenience, we will assume that the original source code and the copy created by the CLM are identical. In other words, the left listing represents the code which the CLM receives as input and at the same time it is the code that will later appear in the code listing display. The source code's jump statements are: the method invocation at line 5 and the *return* statements at the lines 14, 20 and 26. The block statements are: the *if*-statements at lines 4 and 19, and the *while*-statements at lines 9 and 22. All other statements are standard statements. According to our explanation above, the CLM will partition the code

Listing 5.1

Source Code		Simulation Code
``` 1 public BinaryNode successor(BinaryNode x) { 2 3 BinaryNode y = null; 4 if (x.rightChild != null) { 5 y = minimum(x.rightChild); 6 } 7 8 y = x.getParent(); 9 while (y != null && x == y.rightChild) { 10 x = y; 11 y = y.getParent(); 12 } 13 14 return y; 15 } 16 17 private BinaryNode 18 minimum(BinaryNode node) { 19 if (node == null) { 20 return null; 21 } 22 while (node.leftChild != null) { 23 node = node.leftChild; 24 } 25 26 return node; 27 } ```	S1 S2 S3 S4 S5 S6 S7 S8 S9 S10	``` 1 public VisualBinaryNode successor(VisualBinaryNode x) { 2 3 VisualBinaryNode y = null; 4 codeHighlighter.highlightLines(1,4); 5 6 if (x.getRightChild() != null) { 7 codeHighlighter.highlightLines(5,5); 8 y = minimum(x.getRightChild()); 9 } 10 11 y = x.getParentNode(); 12 codeHighlighter.highlightLines(8,9); 13 14 while (y != null && x == y.getRightChild()) { 15 x = y; 16 y = y.getParentNode(); 17 codeHighlighter.highlightLines(10,12); 18 } 19 codeHighlighter.highlightLines(13,15); 20 return y; 21 } 22 23 public VisualBinaryNode minimum(VisualBinaryNode node) { 24 25 codeHighlighter.highlightLines(17,19); 26 27 if (node == null) { 28 codeHighlighter.highlightLines(20,21); 29 return null; 30 } 31 32 codeHighlighter.highlightLines(22,22); 33 34 while (node.getLeftChild() != null) { 35 node = node.getLeftChild(); 36 codeHighlighter.highlightLines(23,24); 37 } 38 39 codeHighlighter.highlightLines(26,27); 40 return node; 41 } ```

Listing 5.1: Set-wise code line mapping

into ten segments. Each segment has been denoted in the listing by framing it in a green rectangle.

Note, that each highlighting statement inserted by the CLM into the simulation code in the right listing (*codeHighlighter.HighlightLines(..)*)corresponds to exactly one segment in the left context. The *highlightLines* method of the highlighter (see right listing) works as follows. It initially unhighlights the currently highlighted lines in the display. Next, it highlights the lines of the passed segment. And finally, it calls an internal wait method. This method pauses the execution of the simulation for a few seconds to enable the user to realise that possibly different lines are highlighted.

5.4.3 Highlighting of pseudo and non-Java code

In the previous subsection, we quietly assumed that the source code passed to the code display is given in Java. We know, however, that novice students are most likely not familiar with the syntax of Java. Further, in Subsection 2.2.2 we required that the source code of the algorithm be displayed in pseudo code notation and in at least one object-oriented-programming language. Assuming that there is a mapping between the simulation code and the Java source code, in order to highlight the lines of the pseudo code, we just need to map each segment of the Java code to its corresponding segment in the pseudo code. Further, we need to modify the implementation of the *highlightLines* method so that it can highlight simultaneously the lines of the Java code, the pseudo code and the codes of the other programming languages, if any. Unfortunately, it is extremely difficult to fully automate the process of mapping the Java source code line segments to their corresponding segments in the pseudo code or codes in other programming languages. Therefore, we perform the mapping manually using a graphical tool called **code mapper** (see Figure 19). We use the code mapper to map each line in the Java code to its corresponding line in the pseudo code and any code expressed in the following supported programming languages: Python, C++, C and C#.

5.5. AUTOMATIC UNDO/REDO

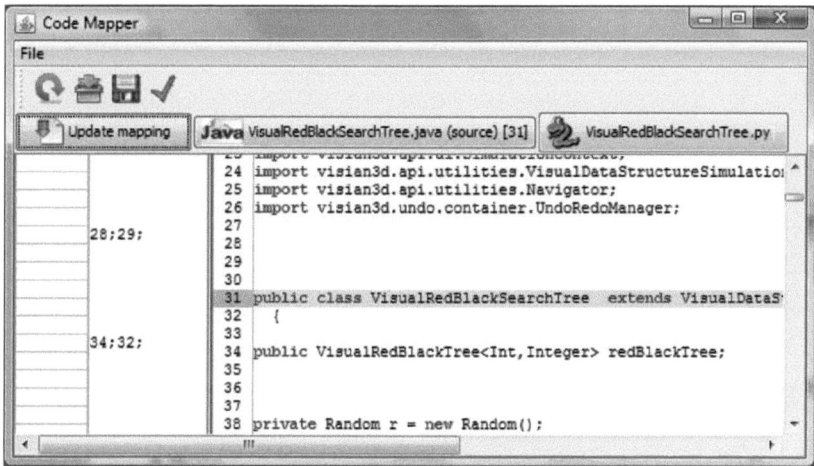

Figure 19: A tool for code listing mapping

5.5 Automatic Undo/Redo

A special attention was given to the development of an automated undo/redo facility, because this greatly facilitates the creation of algorithm visualisations. As previously mentioned, in an internship at our Department of Computer Graphics [54] the students stated that the time needed merely to implement an undo/redo facility was twice as much as the time necessitated to develop the rest of the simulation.

This section introduces an extension of the Java 3D API as an implementation of an efficient undo/redo framework and shows how this framework can be readily used in the automatic creation of three-dimensional visual simulations. The framework uses the memento design pattern to implement a linear multiple-undo/multiple-action model with an unlimited undo of performed actions. In Section 6.4 we will evaluate the framework and discuss its advantages and drawbacks. The work presented here draws on a research that we have recently published in [11].

104 CHAPTER 5. IMPLEMENTATION

In order to ensure a comprehensive understanding of the framework's underlying concept, the reader will initially be made familiar with the basic terminology of Java 3D. Therefore, we will briefly outline the fundamentals of Java 3D in Appendix C.1 and introduce the terms that will be used when explaining the concept in detail. Before proceeding with the remainder of this section, the reader is encouraged to take a quick review through this introduction. For detailed literature, the reader is advised to consult the Java 3D specification [68] or one of the following resources: [108, 119].

5.5.1 Undo design patterns

When developing a concept for an undo/redo facility, there are two design patterns [55] that can be taken into consideration: the memento and the command pattern [53]. The command design pattern is a pattern that enables us to encapsulate each operation (command) that causes changes to the scene graph, into an object called command object. According to this pattern, every change in the state of an application is captured in an undoable command. Reversing the i-th step of an application involves the reversion of all commands generated in step $(i-1)$. The memento design pattern, on the other hand, is a pattern that helps store the recent internal state (memento) of an object and enables the application to restore the object's state later on, if needed. According to the memento pattern, an application consists of a number of objects, each of which has an internal state determined by the occupancy of its fields or the values of its attributes. The state of an application at a specific moment is the overall state of its underlying objects at that moment. An application step i, which commonly consists of a set of actions, transfers the $(i-1)$-th state of the application into state i. Reversing step i requires restoring the application's $(i-1)$-th state.

Both patterns have advantages and disadvantages. In order to decide in favour of one of them, we first need to define some requirements that our concept has to meet:

5.5. AUTOMATIC UNDO/REDO

We require that the concept is generic and allows a straightforward usage of the implemented undo/redo facility and also enables an effortless upgrading of already existing 3D applications. Furthermore, the concept should allow a memory-friendly implementation and support a large number of changes without affecting the application's overall performance or causing memory problems. Being memory-friendly is a very crucial aspect of undo/redo facilities. Since keeping track of the previous changes of an application always requires saving the complete information, the design of memory-friendly undo/redo interfaces has always been considered a huge challenge. In this work, we considered the implementation of both patterns. Implementing the command pattern requires that every action should be encapsulated into a command object and subsequently saved, regardless of whether it affects the scene graph or not [47]. The current release of Java 3D is quite large, and consists of hundreds of classes and interfaces, and thousands of fields and methods. Therefore, the number of actions that can potentially affect the scene graph is enormous. Encapsulating each event into a command object would result in an implementation impossible to handle. Another issue is that there are actions that, in some steps, do not really affect the scene graph. Overriding the geometrical coordinates of a visual object with the same value produces a command which is practically useless for an undo step. Apparently, the command pattern is only geared for applications with a manageable amount of distinct actions. The memento pattern, on the other hand, is straightforward to implement and allows a very efficient and memory-friendly implementation. Therefore, inferring from this observation and from our own experience, we believe that the memento design pattern is more suitable for a wide range of applications than the command pattern. However, it does have a disadvantage that we will explain later in Section 6.4.

5.5.2 Undo model

Apart from a design pattern, an undo/redo concept needs to implement an appropriate undo/redo model. An undo/redo model specifies four aspects of an undo/redo concept: repetition, granularity, limit and linearity. Repetition denotes the number of steps the model allows to be undone. There are single-undo (one step) and multiple-undo (multiple steps). The granularity specifies the number of actions that are allowed to be reversed in each step. If the model allows reversing only one action, it is a single-action model; otherwise it is a multiple-action model. As a consequence of this classification, there are four different undo/redo models: single-undo/single-action, single-undo/multiple-action, multiple-undo/single-action and multiple-undo/multiple-action, each of which can be implemented in a linear or non-linear way. Linear undo requires the user to undo the latest action before undoing earlier ones. With non-linear undo, the actions to be undone can be picked freely from a maintained list of completed actions. In contrast to web browsers, which mostly implement a non-linear model, most text editors support linear undo.

A limited undo/redo model allows for only a limited number of steps to be reversed at once during the execution of the application. An ideal undo/redo concept is one that would support a hybrid unlimited multiple-undo/multiple-action model. Hybrid, in this context, means that the underlying model can be accessed in a linear as well as in a non-linear way. Due to the high flexibility of such a model, it forms the foundation frame of our concept.

5.5.3 Concept fundamentals

Our concept to extend the Java 3D API, so that it can enable a straightforward development of efficient reversible 3D applications, is scene graph-based and independent of the application type. It applies the memento pattern and builds on the following simple thought: We extend the classes of the API and make each of them undoable. An object is undoable if it is capable of sequentially recovering its earlier

5.5. AUTOMATIC UNDO/REDO

states; in other words, when it is able to autonomously reverse any actions that have affected and changed its state. Based on the assumption that the scene graph of an application is assembled from undoable objects, each of which can be reached from the root, the traversing of the scene graph only once, and in doing so requiring each object to restore its, say i-th state, this will result in restoring the entire state of the application at time i.

To become undoable, any scene graph object or a *NodeComponent* in Java 3D is required to implement a specific undoable interface. Figure 20 shows a hierarchy of undoable interfaces that can be implemented by Java 3D classes.

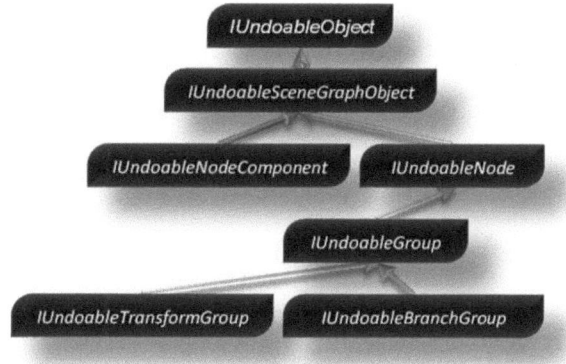

Figure 20: Undoable interface hierarchy

As can be seen, *IUndoableObject* is the super interface of all other undoable interfaces. It defines, among others, the following two methods *saveState()* and *restoreState()*. During the execution, the application is supposed to take a snapshot of the scene graph at the end of each step using a special object called undo/redo manager. To do so, it uses a method called *takeSnapshot()*. The procedure for taking a snapshot is straightforward: whenever a snapshot is to be taken, the undo/redo manager creates a unique snapshot id. It then traverses the scene graph in pre-order starting at its root, visits every node of the scene graph exactly once and requires it to save its current state by invoking its *saveState()* method and

108 CHAPTER 5. IMPLEMENTATION

passing the snapshot id to it.

Each undoable object is expected to implement its own *saveState(snapshotID)* method in such a way that the method saves the values of the object's attributes in special containers (see Subsection 5.5.4). Saving the states of all objects, however, will enable us to restore their previous states, yet not their relation amongst each other, i.e., the structure of the scene graph. Therefore, each time the undo/redo manager traverses the graph, it collects structural information that makes the subsequent rebuilding of its structure possible. This information involves, for example, the id of each group[2] and the types of its children nodes. All of this information is saved in a special data structure called *Snapshot*. When the undo/redo manager creates a snapshot object, it assigns it a unique id and saves it in a special ordered list (see Figure 21). The undo/redo manager is the only object that is allowed

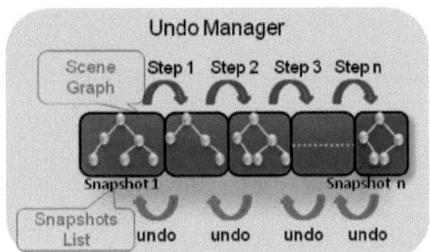

Figure 21: An illustration of the structure of the undo/redo manager

to create snapshot objects. Therefore it is important to stress that a scene graph object does not use instances of the *Snapshot* class to take snapshots of itself, but uses special containers for this purpose instead.

In addition to the structural information, a snapshot object maintains a reference to each node of the scene graph and implements the method *reconstructSceneGraph()*. To reverse the i-th step of the application, the undo/redo manager needs

---

[2]Every undoable scene graph object has a unique id assigned to it at instantiation time. The id of a non-undoable object is its hash code.

5.5. AUTOMATIC UNDO/REDO

to reconstruct the content and structure of the scene graph which was present before executing step $(i+1)$. This is the moment in which a snapshot of the i-th state was taken. To do so, the undo/redo manager invokes *reconstructSceneGraph()* of snapshot i. This method uses the structural information saved in the snapshot object to reconstruct the entire scene graph of step i. During this process, each time a node is added to the graph being reconstructed, this node is required to invoke its own *restoreState()* method. This method replaces the values of the current node's attributes by those which were saved when snapshot i was taken. Listing B.6 in the appendix shows an implementation of the Snapshot class and the recently mentioned methods.

The question that now arises is: When should an application take a snapshot of its scene graph or, in other words, how is an application step to be defined? Actually, this is fully dependent upon the application itself. In fact, it is the task of the application programmer to decide where a step starts and where it terminates. Generally speaking, all actions between two consecutive calls of the *takeSnapshot()* method belong to one and the same step. The first call marks the start and the second call marks the end of the step. In a 3D modelling tool, for example, adding a geometrical primitive should be captured as one step. In a 3D visualisation of a sorting algorithm, swapping two array elements should also be captured in one step. Hence, a snapshot should be taken before and after a complete action.

5.5.4 Undo/Redo containers

As previously mentioned, scene graph objects and *NodeComponents* use special generic data structures called containers to keep track of the values of their fields. Our concept distinguishes between two types of fields: comparable and reference fields. Hence, there are two types of containers: C-containers and R-containers. The former are used to store values of arbitrary comparable data types, i.e. data types which implement the *Comparable*-interface [8]. These can be, characters, strings, numerical types, or others. R-containers, on the other hand, are used to

110 CHAPTER 5. IMPLEMENTATION

keep track of reference values (pointers). For efficiency reasons, there are single and multiple value containers which are used to monitor single or multiple values of several fields simultaneously (see Figure 22). An object can have one or more containers depending on the number and the types of its fields.

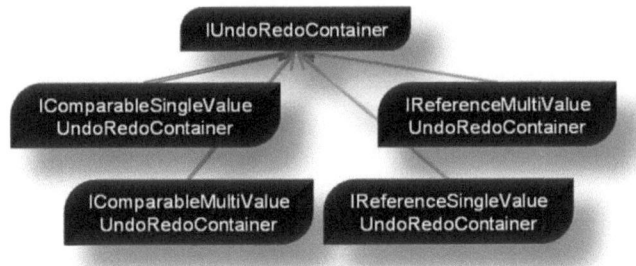

Figure 22: Container interface hierarchy

The most important methods of a single-value container are:

takeSnapshot(int snapshotID, T field), *getSnapshot(int snapshotID)* and *valueChanged(int snapshotID)*, where T is a generic type. The first two methods correspond to the *saveState()* and *restoreState()* methods of the *IUndoableObject* interface, respectively, and are invoked when a scene graph object calls the corresponding method. In other words, the *saveState()* method of an undoable object simply calls *takeSnapshot()* of its container to save its current state. When an object is asked by the undo/redo manager to recover its *i-th* state, it simply invokes the *getSnapshot()* method of its container and overwrites its own current value by the returned one. *valueChanged(snapshotID)* is an essential method which is used to increase the performance of the undo/redo framework. The concept specification requires that when a snapshot of a field in step i is being taken, the current field value is only captured if it differs from the value of step $(i-1)$. Thus, *valueChanged(i)* only returns *true* if the current value of the field and its value in step $(i-1)$ are different. Unless *valueChanged()* returns *true*, no entry is added to the container. This guarantees optimal memory usage and contributes to the fulfilment of our initial demand for a memory-friendly implementation.

Moreover, containers can be deactivated. The application can invoke the *setActive()* method of the *IUndoRedoContainer* interface to activate and deactivate a container. As long as a container is inactive, it will not be able to take further snapshots of its fields. This is a very useful feature, particularly when an application knows that the values of some fields monitored by a container will not change after a particular step.

5.6 An Algorithm Visualisation Environment

The environment we are presenting now is composed of an algorithm visualisation programming interface (VPI), an algorithm visualisation platform and a code generator (CG). The latter has already been presented in Section 5.3. The VPI is a rich collection of Java and Java 3D classes, which are arranged in several packages and serve as a library for developing algorithm visualisations. It contains a large number of implementations of reusable components and visual objects. Unless this VPI is provided, visualisations are often arduous and difficult to design and implement. It ensures that programmers do not need to reinvent or reimplement facilities common to all or most simulations.

There are two types of components available in the VPI, which can be borrowed by all simulations — graphical and non-graphical components. The graphical components are either visual components implemented in Swing [118], such as graphical views, text displays, control panels, icon bars, tabs, etc., or visual objects implemented in Java 3D, such as visual arrays, graphs, trees, data structure editors, etc. The non-graphical components include input validators, scanners for syntax colouring, code parsers, and many other components. In the following section we will elaborate on the platform and describe its fundamental architecture.

5.7 3D-Visian — An Algorithm Visualisation Platform

3D-Visian stands for "three-dimensional **Vi**sual **Si**mulation and **An**imation of algorithms" and denotes a general purpose platform for the development and deployment of 3D algorithm visualisations. It acts primarily as an execution environment for any kind of visualisations, especially 2D and 3D visual simulations and passive animations. In contrast to many AV systems, 3D-Visian is not domain-specific. It is a universal system in the sense that it allows the visualisation of algorithms of any topic related to computer science, computer graphics, bioinformatics, chemistry or any other field. This is due to its visualisation-independent and extensible architecture, which we will introduce in the following subsection (see also [14]).

5.7.1 System Architecture

In order for an AVS to be applied as an effective e-learning and teaching system, it needs to meet two fundamental requirements which concern the domain and the type of the visualisations:

- The system should be domain-independent and applicable for the visualisation of algorithms of any field.

- The system should allow any type of visualisation, especially interactive and passive animations.

The key idea to meet these requirements is to decouple the implementation of the system from the implementation of the visualisations. To achieve this, we defined an extensible set of predefined interfaces. To be executable in 3D-Visian, a visualisation is obliged to implement one of these interfaces. Implementation in this context means that the visualisation should provide a concrete implementation for each method included in the interface.

5.7. 3D-VISIAN — AN ALGORITHM VISUALISATION PLATFORM

At the same time, for each interface there is a corresponding graphical user interface or UI for short, which is incorporated in the system. The UI is the graphical component of the system that allows the user to control and interact with the visualisation via the interface. It consists of simple widgets, such as input fields and buttons that provide the user with the ability to influence the animation flow (see Figure 23). Whenever a visualisation that implements an interface is about to be loaded into the system, the corresponding graphical user interface is automatically loaded and placed as a control bar at the bottom of the system's frame (see Figures 23 and 24 below). Each widget in the UI is linked to a method in the interface. When the user clicks on a button or a field in the UI, the corresponding method of the visualisation will be invoked. Note that for all visualisations that implement the same interface, there is only one instance of the UI and not one instance for each. The question that now arises is: How are these interfaces to be defined?

In order to support an unlimited domain of algorithm visualisations, we utilised a simple method to group algorithms and data structures into classes. Each class includes only algorithms or data structures (or both) which can be controlled by the same graphical user interface. To clarify the basic concept behind the architecture, we will take two classes of algorithms and data structures as an example:

According to our concept, conventional algorithms such as sorting, graph, and matrix calculation algorithms form the first class, denoted as C_a. This is because the execution of these algorithms can be controlled in the same manner. The corresponding user interface provides controls for starting, stopping, pausing the animation, and playing it backwards and forwards either in stepwise or continuous mode, as can be seen in Figure 23.

Figure 23: A graphical user interface for C_a

A second group of algorithms contains tree-like data structures, such as Binary, AVL, Splay, (a,b) and red-black trees, which all fall into the second class, denoted as C_b. The UI for this class consists of one input field and many control buttons for performing the typical operations of these data structures, such as *insert*, *delete* and *lookup* in addition to *undo* and *redo* (see Figure 24).

Figure 24: A graphical user interface for C_b

Again, according to the concept, all algorithm visualisations of the same class must implement a programming interface which includes among others methods that correspond to the UI's widgets. The programming interface for class C_a, for example, contains the following methods: *start()*, *stop()*, *nextStep()*, *previousStep()*, *pause()*, *forward()* and *backward()*. The interface of C_b includes accordingly, an *insert()*, a *delete()*, a *lookup()*, an *undo()* and a *redo()* method.

In order for a visualisation to be loaded into the system, it must additionally provide a simple text file called vis-file, which contains the name of the main-class (the starting point of the visualisation). The visualisation classes together with the vis-file do not have to be stored on the same machine as the system. They can be stored locally in the file system or on any other host. For example, a student in South Africa who has developed their own visualisation and stored it on their university's host, can start the system, which is hosted on a remote server in Germany via the Internet, and use it at home to load their visualisation, or even a visualisation developed by a student in the United States and stored on yet another host, simply by typing the URI of the corresponding vis-file. The facilities for web access to visualisations are managed by the system.

Another remarkable feature of the system is its ability to load and execute several visualisations simultaneously. Each visualisation is loaded into a separate tab and has its own user control interface. An illustration of the architecture can be seen in Figure 25. A simple evaluation of the system can be found in Section 6.5. The reader is invited to explore the system by visiting the following location [2].

5.7. 3D-VISIAN — AN ALGORITHM VISUALISATION PLATFORM

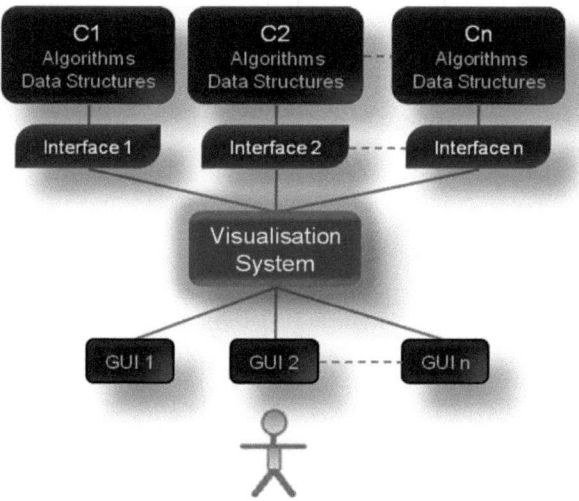

Figure 25: A simple illustration of the architecture of 3D-Visian

Chapter 6

Summary, Evaluation and Perspectives on Future Work

Simply claiming that a certain research is a success, is less than convincing unless this claim is substantiated by an evaluation.

In addition to a summary, this concluding chapter contains an overall evaluation of the entire work. Some of the sections evaluate the semi-automatic approach, the approach for the animation of computational-intensive algorithms, the undo/redo framework and 3D-Visian. Each evaluation starts by listing the advantages and concludes with discussing any drawbacks. Finally, we will call the reader's attention to an unexplored research area.

6.1 Summary

Motivated by a deep conviction that visual algorithm simulations are a powerful means to overcome problems that arise when studying and teaching the abstract aspects of algorithms, and believing that current techniques to craft meaningful algorithm visualisations are far from being practical and efficient, we launched this research to investigate, identify and break through the obstacles that make the development of algorithm visualisation such a hard task. In the introductory chapter we defined the terminology associated with the field of software and algorithm visualisation, and gave an overview of a couple of representative algorithm visualisation systems in addition to a survey of the state of the art in this research area. We next discussed the motivating problems of our research and defined the objectives of this work. In Chapter 2 we presented some development and design aspects of algorithm visualisations, such as 2D vs 3D visualisations and the importance of using a uniform design style when designing algorithm visualisation. Next, we defined a list of requirements we seek to meet when developing algorithm visualisations, introduced the term "hybrid simulations"; made a proposal for the parties involved in developing algorithm simulations and presented a workflow for developing the anticipated visual simulations. Later, we investigated whether or not there is a link between the common design paradigms Greedy-Algorithms, Divide-&-Conquer and Dynamic-Programming, and the visualisation complexity of algorithms. To explore the issues concerning the automation of algorithm simulations we investigated a large number of algorithms and examined them in respect to automation. Through this investigation, we gained an insight into a number of intricate problems that made the automation complexity much more apparent. This finding lead us to develop an approach to partially automate the process of creating visual simulations instead of automating the visualisation process itself. The approach is based on three concepts: visual objects, code augmentation and reusable parameterised components. We then went a step further and presented an approach for animating computation-intensive 3D algorithms and 3D algorithms for $\mathcal{NP}$-complete problems, which by nature cannot be simulated for arbitrary input length. Further, we developed a clustering-based approach for facilitating the development of parallel algorithms. Finally, in an implementation chapter, we covered the implementation aspects of our approach and presented a powerful scene graph-based API for equipping algorithm visualisations with undo/redo facilities. Additionally, we presented an environment for three-dimensional visualisations of arbitrary algorithms and data structures. The environment consists of three major units: An algorithm visualisation programming interface (VPI), a code generator (CG), and an algorithm visualisation system (AVS) called 3D-Visian. We now evaluate our work and conclude this thesis with a brief discussion on a topic for future research.

6.2 Evaluation of the Approach

The approach introduced in Section 4.2 is intuitive, serves its purpose, and allows for generating arbitrary simulations with an expandable number of requirements. It however, suffers from a serious disadvantage: The approach is based on the notion of exploiting synergies in the development process. The more algorithms there are that share the same data structures (visual objects) and reusable components, the higher the synergies. This is because for each group of algorithms that share the same data structures — and hence similar operations — it was necessary to encapsulate the structures into visual objects and implement their operations only once. All group members can later share these implementations. However, once we encountered an algorithm with an 'extraordinary' data structure, initially we were forced to implement this data structure as a visual object, and to make it available in the VPI, before being able to use it. Additionally, we had to extend the code generator and make it familiar with this new object. This is often the case with computer graphics algorithms. Most computer graphics algorithms, we have worked with so far have little in common. Moreover, they have proven to gain little from this approach. We conjecture that this will also be the case with bioinformatics algorithms.

6.3 Evaluation of the Approach for Animating Algorithms to $\mathcal{NP}$-Complete Problems

Despite all the disadvantages of passive animations, this kind of graphical presentation is the only possibility to visualise computation-intensive algorithms and algorithms to $\mathcal{NP}$-complete problems (ANPP). In our opinion, non-computation-intensive algorithms should only be visualised using real-time simulations. As mentioned earlier, algorithm animation languages are not the only way to create passive animations of algorithms. High-level programming languages can also be used for this purpose. However, both alternatives have their own advantages and drawbacks. One of the advantages of applying animation languages is that no programming skills are required for designing animations. For example, novice students and designers without any programming skills can create professional and visually attractive animations that comply with many design guidelines [107], whereas the use of programming languages requires both design and programming experience. This allows animation authors to focus on the didactical and design aspects of the animation. On the other hand, high-level programming languages are more powerful than algorithm animation languages, as the latter normally support neither loops nor conditional assignments. The question that arises is whether to use a high-level programming language or an algorithm animation language to animate a given algorithm or data structure. To answer this question, we now examine another example of a computation-intensive and graphically demanding bioinformatics algorithm.

The iterated loop matching algorithm (ILMA) [70] is a bioinformatics algorithm, which can predict the RNA secondary structure including pseudo knots. It is based on the loop matching algorithm introduced by Nussinov et al. [86], which uses dynamic-programming as well as thermodynamic and comparative (covariance) information. This algorithm can predict any type of pseudo knots both in aligned and single-stranded sequences. The worst-case running time of the ILM algorithm is $O(n^4)$, where n is the length of the input sequence. Figure 26 shows a segment of

6.3. EVALUATION OF THE APPROACH FOR ANIMATING ALGORITHMS TO $\mathcal{NP}$-COMPLETE PROBLEMS

an animation of this algorithm implemented using a script programming language[1].

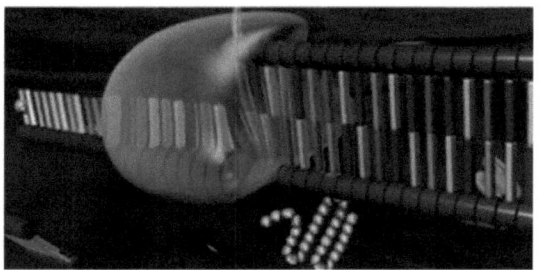

Figure 26: A segment of an RNA animation

Obviously such graphically demanding algorithms cannot be efficiently visualised using an algorithm animation language, regardless of how powerful the language is.

Theoretically, each algorithm can be visualised using a powerful 3D algorithm animation language, but the question is: To what degree of effort and quality. In our opinion, such kinds of algorithms can only be reasonably visualised in a high-level programming language. The creation of computation-intensive algorithms using an algorithm animation language is at least as complex as using a high-level programming language, and in some cases, e.g., the travelling-salesman problem, requires almost as much programming skills. Therefore, we consider the approach of creating computation-intensive algorithms using an algorithm animation language as impractical and inefficient. Even if we had used tools like XML editors to generate the 1873 lines of our TSP example, the computation of the intermediate steps would still be unavoidable. Therefore, we recommend the use of high-level programming languages for both passive animations and dynamic simulations of algorithms.

---

[1]Source: http://www.youtube.com/watch?v=Ml0OqAUzEXU and http://rufusrajadurai.wetpaint.com/?t=anon

6.4 Evaluation of the Undo/Redo Facility

The introduced concept and its implementation, as an extension of the Java 3D API, have both advantages and drawbacks. Perhaps one of the greatest advantages of the concept is that it is scene graph-based. This means that it can be applied to any scene graph-based 3D API, such as OGRE [87], OpenSceneGraph [88], etc. Furthermore, the resulted API is not restricted to a particular application type. It can be used to implement an undo/redo functionality for an arbitrary 3D application at minimal effort. Another key advantage of the concept lies in its memory-friendly and efficient implementation. When a snapshot of the scene graph is being taken, only values of fields which have changed in the most recent step are saved. Applications with little changes to the scene graph will only consume a little memory. Moreover, the containers can be switched on and off at any time. Deactivating a container is particularly useful when changes to the values of fields maintained by the container are irrelevant and can be ignored, or when the application knows that the values of the fields are not going to change after a particular step. This will make it unnecessary to attempt to compare all recent values with the previous ones, to find out whether they have changed or not. For example, when comparing two (4 × 4) transformation matrices of an *UndoableTransformGroup*, deactivating a container will save up to 16 floating point comparisons, thus reducing the impact that the undo/redo feature has on the application runtime.

Taking a snapshot of the scene graph requires traversing the entire graph only once in each step. This can be achieved in $\Theta(n)$ where n represents the number of the graph nodes plus the objects they are referencing (the *NodeComponents*). When one considers that the renderer of the Java 3D API traverses the scene graph continuously in a loop to update scene graph changes, one can then infer that one additional cycle in each step will definitely not slow down the application. The objects of a 3D scene are never cloned. Each object exists only once. Keeping track of an object is realised by using references/pointers to it. A reference in Java or

6.4. EVALUATION OF THE UNDO/REDO FACILITY

Application	Number of undoable objects	0 steps	20 steps	40 steps	60 steps	80 steps	100 steps
1.	1000	1.7 MB	3.0 MB	4.2 MB	5.9 MB	7.2 MB	8.6 MB
2.	2000	3.4 MB	5.9 MB	8.7 MB	11.5 MB	14.2 MB	17.2 MB
3.	5000	8.2 MB	15.4 MB	21.75 MB	28.9 MB	35.6 MB	43.3 MB

Table 5: Memory consumption of three distinct applications

a pointer in C++ is usually either represented by four or eight bytes, depending upon whether the underlying operating system is a 32 or 64-bit-system. It can be easily shown that saving the additional structural information that is essential for reconstructing the scene graph, only requires saving $2m + k$ id's, where m is the number of the leafs of the graph and k the number of its inner nodes. Expressed in asymptotic notation, $2m+k$ is equivalent to $\Theta(n)$ references. Hence, the additional memory consumption remains linear in regards to the size of the scene graph. We use integers as keys to uniquely identify undoable objects. Integers in Java and C++ are four bytes. Table 5 demonstrates the growth of the memory consumption of three distinct applications with different amounts of undoable objects.

Figure 27 illustrates the memory consumption of a reversible application using 2300 undoable objects after taking 100 snapshots. After analysing the memory consumption of several applications, it turned out that the memory usage in each step increases by 0.0063% on average per undoable object.

The undo/redo manager maintains an ordered list for arranging the snapshots of the graph. Accessing the list chronologically results in an implementation of the linear undo/redo model, accessing it randomly, using the snapshot ids, will result in an implementation of a non-linear undo/redo model. Hence, the implemented undo/redo model is hybrid and, due to its memory-friendly implementation, supports an unlimited amount of reversals. The usage of the undo/redo API is straightforward. An application needs to create an instance of the undo/redo manager and make it globally available. Whenever an undoable object is needed, the application creates an instance of the corresponding class, sets its capabilities, and invokes its *initContainers()* method prior to adding it to the scene graph. At the end of each

124   CHAPTER 6. SUMMARY, EVALUATION AND PERSPECTIVES

step the application needs to invoke the *takeSnapshot()* method in order to enable the undoing of this step later on.

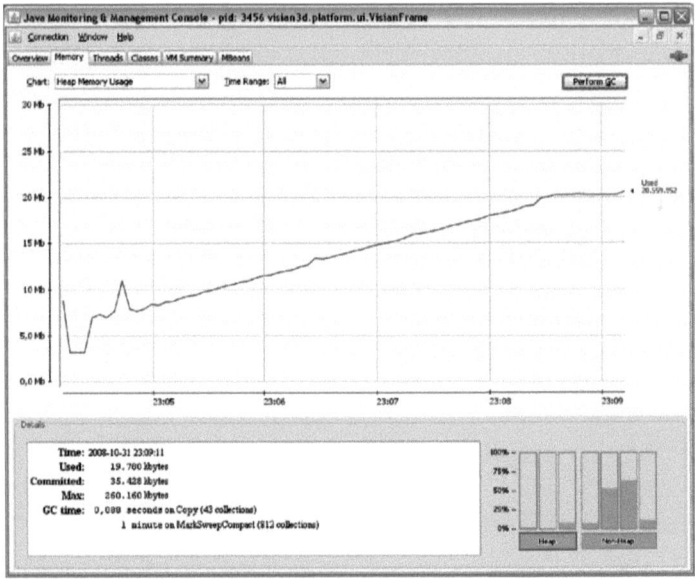

Figure 27: Memory consumption of an application with 2300 objects after 100 steps

To reverse a step, the application merely needs to call the *undo()* method of the undo/redo manager when it wants to have a linear undo/redo, or it invokes *restoreSnapshot(snapshotID)* when it wants to apply a non-linear undo/redo.

Redoing a step is achieved by calling either the *redo()* or the *restoreSnapshot(snapshotID)* method. An application can have a mixture of undoable and non-undoable objects. This makes upgrading earlier applications straightforward. Replacing undoable objects can be done simply by using the find & replace feature of an IDE editor.

Despite all of these advantages, this concept suffers from some drawbacks. The major disadvantage of the concept is related to the usage of the memento pattern. Using the snapshot approach makes undo steps become static. Reversing

6.4. EVALUATION OF THE UNDO/REDO FACILITY

animated actions happens in a discrete unanimated way. For example, when an application utilises an animation to smoothly move an object from position p_1 to position p_3 via an intermediate position p_2, the undo/redo manager undoes this action by instantly putting the object to its original position (p_1). This problem, however, can be solved by combining the memento pattern with an implementation of the command pattern which then enables a smooth reversal of animated actions. A further disadvantage is, that whenever a snapshot is being taken, each active container performs one comparison for each field it maintains, in order to decide whether the value of the field has changed or not. This costs runtime. However, if the runtime performance of an application is more important than the memory consumption, then the application developer can overwrite the containers, so that the current field value is not compared to the previous value and is always saved, regardless of whether it has changed or not. There is another disadvantage, which actually relates to a restriction in some 3D APIs, such as Java 3D. Children of compiled groups are not allowed to be detached. To reconstruct the scene graph of step i, however, each group child must be detached from its current parent and attached to the parent it had at time i. This is because the undo/redo manager always operates on the objects themselves and does not create duplicates of them. Therefore, none of the descendants of a scene graph object that are in the path from the object to the scene graph root, are allowed to be compiled. According to the Java 3D specification, compiling a group object increases the performance of the application. The specification, however, does not comprehensively specify at what level it might affect the overall performance of the application. There is another issue relative to the maintenance of the API. The implementation of the undo/redo concept is entirely based on the current release of the used API. Future releases of the API, which include new objects, require upgrading of the current implementation. Changes to the API implementation, such as deprecating fields, methods or classes might force a slight adaptation of the current implementation.

Nevertheless, we do believe that our framework will aid many 3D application developers in creating new reversible applications and upgrading earlier ones.

6.5 Evaluation of 3D-Visian

As mentioned previously, 3D-Visian is not domain-specific. This was made possible by decoupling the implementation of the visualisations from the system's implementation. It is extensible, as it allows defining new interfaces and thus providing visualisation support to new classes of algorithms. Once a new class, say for the visual simulation of formal languages and automata, needs to be supported, simply a new interface should be defined and linked to a conforming graphical user interface. The disadvantage of partially implementing the system and the VPI in Java 3D is that only developers with more or less advanced Java 3D skills are able to produce their own simulations. Further, users of the system must have Java 3D installed on their client, which might limit the range of users. If this is not the case, integrated routines can recognise this and offer the user an automatic installation. The reader is invited to evaluate the system by themselves by launching it from the following location [2].

6.6 Future Work

Our research has concentrated on creating adaptable algorithm simulations; in other words, simulations that can be adapted by the user to their own level of knowledge. Much more research can be conducted to develop adaptive algorithm simulations. That is, simulations that can autonomously adapt themselves to the user's level of knowledge in direct response to their learning progress. This is an unexplored area in the world of algorithm visualisation which requires the employment of methods from the field of artificial intelligence.

Bibliography

[1] InfoVis 2009. http://vis.computer.org/VisWeek2009/infovis/papers.html.

[2] 3D-Visian. http://www.3dvisian.de.

[3] Alfred Aho, Ravi Sathi and Jeffrey Ullman. *Compilers, Principles, Techniques, and Tools*. Addison-Wesley, 1986.

[4] Janet E. Finlay (and Gregory D. Abowd Alan J. Dix (Author), Russell Beale and Janet E. Finley. *Human-Computer Interaction*. Prentice Hall, 3 edition edition, 2003.

[5] Java Annotations. http://java.sun.com/docs/books/tutorial/java/javaOO/annotations.html.

[6] Craig Anslow, James Noble, Stuart Marshall and Robert Biddle. X3D Web Based Algorithm Animation, 2007.

[7] Craig Anslow, James Noble, Stuart Marshall and Robert Biddle. X3D Web Based Algorithm Animation. In *Technical Report CS-TR-07/1*, May 2007.

[8] Java API. http://download.java.net/jdk7/docs/api/.

[9] Java3D API. https://java3d.dev.java.net. Sun Microsystems.

[10] Ronald Baecker. Sorting Out Sorting: A Case Study of Software Visualization for Teaching Computer Science. In *Software Visualization: Programming as a Multimedia Experience, chapter 24*, pages 369–381. The MIT Press, 1998.

[11] Ashraf Abu Baker. An Efficient Undo/Redo-Framework for Three-Dimensional Visual Simulation of Algorithms and Data Structures. *GRAPP (to appear) http://grapp.org/GRAPP2009/*, February 2009.

[12] Ashraf Abu Baker, Dirk Grunwald and Stefan Kappes. XML-based Three-Dimensional Animation of Algorithms and Data Structures (In German). In *DeLFI*, pages 401–412, 2008.

[13] Ashraf Abu Baker and Stefan Kappes. Three-Dimensional Static Animation of Computation-Intensive 3D-Algorithms. In *IEEE-CSSE (5)*, pages 434–437. IEEE Computer Society, 2008.

[14] Ashraf Abu Baker and Boris Milanovic. A Universal Extensible Architecture for Algorithm Visualisation Systems. In *IEEE-CSSE (5)*, pages 737–740. IEEE Computer Society, 2008.

[15] Ashraf Abu Baker and Alexander Tillmann. Ein generisches Konzept zur Realisierung von Self-Assessments zur Studienwahl und Selbsteinschätzung der Studierfähigkeit (In German). In *DeLFI*, pages 79–90, 2007.

[16] Ashraf Abu Baker, Alexander Tillmann and Detlef Krömker. Conception, Implementation and Evaluation of Self-Assessments. *The International Conference on Technology, Communication & Education, IEEE-I-CTE 2008*, April 2008.

[17] Ashraf Abu Baker, Alexander Tillmann and Detlef Krömker. Using Self-Assessments for Predicting the Success of Study. *Information and Communication Technologies: From Theory to Applications, 2008. IEEE-ICTTA 2008. 3rd International Conference on Information & Communication Technologies*, pages 1–5, April 2008.

[18] J. Timothy Baker. Three dimensional mesh generation by triangulation of arbitrary point sets. *Computational Fluid Dynamics Conference*, Number 8, pages 255–271, June 1987.

[19] D. Bertsekas and J.N. Tsitsiklis. Parallel and Distributed Computation. In *Numerical Methods*. Prentice Hall, 1989.

[20] Peter Biela. Simple 3D Data Structure Editor (Master's thesis in German). *Department of Computer Science and Mathematics, Goethe Universität Frankfurt/Main*, April 2008.

[21] Christopher M. Boroni, Frances W. Goosey, Michael T. Grinder and Rockford J. Ross. Engaging students with active learning resources: hypertextbooks for the web. *SIGCSE Bull.*, Volume 33, Number 1, pages 65–69, 2001.

[22] Paul Bourke. The shortest line between two lines in 3D. http://local.wasp.uwa.edu.au/p̄bourke/geometry/lineline3d/.

[23] M. H. Brown and M. A. Najork. Algorithm animation using 3D interactive graphics. In *UIST '93: Proceedings of the 6th annual ACM symposium on User interface software and technology*, pages 93–100, New York, NY, USA, 1993. ACM.

[24] M. H. Brown and M. A. Najork. Algorithm Animation Using 3D Interactive Graphics. *ACM Symposium on User Interface Software and Technology*, pages 93–100, Nov 1993.

[25] Marc Brown. *Algorithm Animation*. Ph.D. thesis, Computer Science Department, Brown University, 1986.

[26] M.H. Brown and R. Sedgewick. A System for Algorithm Animation. *ACM SIGCSE*, pages 177–186, July 1984.

[27] Erick Clayberg and Dan Rubel. *Eclipse —Building Commercial-Quality Plugins*. Addison Wesley, second edition edition, 2002.

[28] Java comments. http://java.sun.com/docs/codeconv/html/CodeConventions.doc4.html.

130 BIBLIOGRAPHY

[29] Java3D Community. http://www.j3d.org/.

[30] Arturo I. Concepcion, Nathan Leach and Allan Knight. Algorithma 99: an experiment in reusability & component based software engineering. *SIGCSE Bull.*, Volume 32, Number 1, pages 162–166, 2000.

[31] Thomas H. Cormen, Charles E. Leiserson, Ronald L. Rivest and Clifford Stein. Introduction to Algorithms. pages 258–259, Cambridge, 2002. The MIT press.

[32] Thomas H. Cormen, Charles E. Leiserson, Ronald L. Rivest and Clifford Stein. Introduction to Algorithms/ Convex Hull. pages 947–957, Cambridge, 2002. The MIT press.

[33] Thomas H. Cormen, Charles E. Leiserson, Ronald L. Rivest and Clifford Stein. Introduction to Algorithms/ DFS. pages 540–549, Cambridge, 2002. The MIT press.

[34] Thomas H. Cormen, Charles E. Leiserson, Ronald L. Rivest and Clifford Stein. Introduction to Algorithms/ Dijkstra. pages 595–599, Cambridge, 2002. The MIT press.

[35] Thomas H. Cormen, Charles E. Leiserson, Ronald L. Rivest and Clifford Stein. Introduction to Algorithms/ Floyd-Warshall algorithm. pages 629–632, Cambridge, 2002. The MIT press.

[36] Thomas H. Cormen, Charles E. Leiserson, Ronald L. Rivest and Clifford Stein. Introduction to Algorithms/ Huffman Code. pages 385–391, Cambridge, 2002. The MIT press.

[37] Thomas H. Cormen, Charles E. Leiserson, Ronald L. Rivest and Clifford Stein. Introduction to Algorithms/ Insertion Sort. pages 15–19, Cambridge, 2002. The MIT press.

[38] Thomas H. Cormen, Charles E. Leiserson, Ronald L. Rivest and Clifford Stein. Introduction to Algorithms/ Interval Scheduling. pages 399–402, Cambridge, 2002. The MIT press.

[39] Thomas H. Cormen, Charles E. Leiserson, Ronald L. Rivest and Clifford Stein. Introduction to Algorithms/ Left-Rotate. pages 277–278, Cambridge, 2002. The MIT press.

[40] Thomas H. Cormen, Charles E. Leiserson, Ronald L. Rivest and Clifford Stein. Introduction to Algorithms/ Longest Common Sequence. pages 629–632, Cambridge, 2002. The MIT press.

[41] Thomas H. Cormen, Charles E. Leiserson, Ronald L. Rivest and Clifford Stein. Introduction to Algorithms/ Matrix-Multiplication. pages 756–758, Cambridge, 2002. The MIT press.

[42] Thomas H. Cormen, Charles E. Leiserson, Ronald L. Rivest and Clifford Stein. Introduction to Algorithms/ Red-Black Trees. pages 273–301, Cambridge, 2002. The MIT press.

[43] Thomas H. Cormen, Charles E. Leiserson, Ronald L. Rivest and Clifford Stein. Introduction to Algorithms/ String Matching. pages 906–922, Cambridge, 2002. The MIT press.

[44] Thomas H. Cormen, Charles E. Leiserson, Ronald L. Rivest and Clifford Stein. Introduction to Algorithms/ The algorithms of Kruskal and Prim. pages 567–573, Cambridge, 2002. The MIT press.

[45] Thomas H. Cormen, Charles E. Leiserson, Ronald L. Rivest and Clifford Stein. Introduction to Algorithms/ TSP. pages 1027–1032, Cambridge, 2002. The MIT press.

[46] Martha E. Crosby and Jan Stelovsky. From multimedia instruction to multimedia evaluation. *J. Educ. Multimedia Hypermedia*, Volume 4, Number 2-3, pages 147–162, 1995.

[47] Sandjo Wacka Orphee Cyrille. Conception and Implemention of an Undo/Redo-Manager for Algorithm Simulations (Master's thesis in German). *Department of Computer Science and Mathematics, Goethe Universität Frankfurt/Main*, March 2008.

[48] Voronoi Diagram. http://en.wikipedia.org/wiki/Voronoi_diagram.

[49] Stefan Diehl. *Software Visualization*. Springer Verlag, Berlin Heidelberg, 1997.

[50] Eclipse. http://www.eclipse.org/.

[51] J. Foley, A. van Dam, S. Feiner and J. Hughes. *Computer Graphics: Principles and Practice in C*. Addison Wesley.

[52] J. Foley, A. van Dam, S. Feiner and J. Hughes. *Computer Graphics: Principles and Practice in C/ Ray Tracing*. Addison Wesley.

[53] E. Freeman, K. Sierra and B. Bates. *Head First Design Patterns*. O'Reilly, 2004.

[54] Professur für Graphische Datenverarbeitung. http://www.gdv.informatik.uni-frankfurt.de/.

[55] E. Gamma, R. Helm, R. Johnson and J. Vlissides. *Design Patterns: Elements of Reusable Object-Oriented Software*. Addison-Wesley, 1994.

[56] Michael R. Garey and David S. Johnson. *Computers and Intractability; A Guide to the Theory of NP-Completeness*. W. H. Freeman & Co., New York, NY, USA, 1990.

[57] P. Gloor. Animated algorithms. In *Software visualisation: Programming as a multimedia experience*, pages 409–416, MA, 1998. MIT Press.

[58] Herman H. Goldstein and John von Neumann. Planning and coding of problems for an electronic computing instrument. In *DAC '01: Proceedings of*

the *38th conference on Design automation*, pages 80–151, Taub, 1947. von Neumann's Collected Works.

[59] Mordecai Golin, Rajeev Raman, Christian Schwarz and Michiel Smid. Simple randomized algorithms for closest pair problems. *Nordic J. of Computing*, Volume 2, Number 1, pages 3–27, 1995.

[60] Dirk Grunwald. *3D Animation und Visualisierung von Algorithmen (Master's thesis in German)*. Department of Computer Science and Mathematics, Goethe Universität Frankfurt/Main, Dec. 2007.

[61] Judith Susan Gurka. *Pedagogic aspects of algorithm animation*. Ph.D. thesis, Boulder, CO, USA, 1996. Director-Citrin, Wayne.

[62] S. Hansen, N. Narayanan and D. Schrimpsher. Helping learners visualize and comprehend algorithms., 2000. Interactive Multimedia Electronic Journal of Computer-Enhanced Learning.

[63] Imad Hassani. Semi-automatische Generierung von didaktischen Hilfsmittel in einem generischen Algorithmenvisualisierungssystem (Master's thesis in German). *Department of Computer Science and Mathematics, Goethe Universität Frankfurt/Main*, May 2008.

[64] Vlastimil Havran, Jimí Bittner and Jimi Sára. Ray Tracing with Rope Trees. In László Szirmay Kalos (editor), *14th Spring Conference on Computer Graphics*, pages 130–140, 1998.

[65] C. Hundhausen, S. Douglasw and A. Staskoz. A Meta-Study of Algorithm Visualization Effectiveness, Journal of Visual Languages and Computing.

[66] Janet M. Incerpi. *A Study of the Worst-Case Behavior of Shell-Sort*. Ph.D. thesis, Computer Science Department, Brown University, 1986.

[67] Joseph Jaja. *An Introduction to Parallel Algorithms*. Addison-Wesley Professional, March 1992.

[68] JavaSoft. *The Java 3D API Specification*. Sun Microsystems, http://dlc.sun.com/pdf/806-5414-10/806-5414-10.pdf, 2000.

[69] Jeliot. http://cs.joensuu.fi/jeliot/.

[70] Yongmei Ji, Xing Xu and Gary D. Stormo. A graph theoretical approach for predicting common RNA secondary structure motifs including pseudoknots in unaligned sequences. *Bioinformatics*, Volume 20, Number 10, pages 1591–1602, 2004.

[71] JSAMBA. http://gvu.cc.gatech.edu/softviz/algoanim/jsamba.

[72] LEE C. K. Automatic metric 3D surface mesh generation using subdivision surface geometrical model. *International journal for numerical methods in engineering*, Volume 56, Number 11, pages 1593–1614, 2003.

[73] Ville Karavirta, Ari Korhonen, Lauri Malmi and Kimmo Stalnacke. Matrix-Pro - A Tool for Demonstrating Data Structures and Algorithms Ex Tempore. In *ICALT '04: Proceedings of the IEEE International Conference on Advanced Learning Technologies*, pages 892–893, Washington, DC, USA, 2004. IEEE Computer Society.

[74] Al Khwarizmi. http://de.wikipedia.org/wiki/Al-Chwarizmi.

[75] Al Khwarizmi. http://www.biographybase.com/biography/Al_Khwarizmi.html.

[76] Kenneth Knowlton. http://www.knowltonmosaics.com/.

[77] Kenneth Knowlton. The Beflix Movie Language. Technical report, Proceedings of the Spring Joint Computer Conference, 1964.

[78] Donald E. Knuth. Dynamic Huffman Coding. *Journal of Algorithms*, Volume 6, Number 2, pages 163–180, June 1985.

[79] A. Lawrence. *Empirical studies of the value of algorithm animation in algorithm understanding*. Ph.D. thesis, Department of Computer Science, Georgia Institute of Technology, 1993.

[80] Maksim Mosgowoi. Visuelle Simulation paralleler Algorithmen (Master's thesis in German). *Department of Computer Science and Mathematics, Goethe Universität Frankfurt/Main*, August 2008.

[81] S. Näher. *The Travelling-salesman problem (In German)*. http://www-i1.informatik.rwth-aachen.de/, 2006.

[82] M. A. Najork and M. H. Brown. Web-based algorithm animation. In *DAC '01: Proceedings of the 38th conference on Design automation*, pages 506–511, New York, NY, USA, 2001. ACM.

[83] Thomas L. Naps, James R. Eagan and Laura L. Norton. JHAVÉ—an environment to actively engage students in Web-based algorithm visualizations. *SIGCSE Bull.*, Volume 32, Number 1, pages 109–113, 2000.

[84] Thomas L. Naps, Guido Rößling, Vicki Almstrum, Wanda Dann, Rudolf Fleischer, Chris Hundhausen, Ari Korhonen, Lauri Malmi, Myles McNally, Susan Rodger and J. Ángel Velázquez-Iturbide. Exploring the role of visualization and engagement in computer science education. In *ITiCSE-WGR '02: Working group reports from ITiCSE on Innovation and technology in computer science education*, pages 131–152, New York, NY, USA, 2002. ACM.

[85] Isaac Nassi and Ben Shneiderman. Flowchart techniques for structured programming. *SIGPLAN Notices*, Volume 8, Number 8, pages 12–26, August 1973.

[86] R. Nussinov and A. B. Jacobson. Fast algorithm for predicting the secondary structure of single-stranded RNA. *Proceedings of the National Academy of Science of the USA*, Volume 77, Number 11, pages 1591–1602, 1980.

[87] Ogre. http://www.ogre3d.org.

[88] OpenSceneGraph. http://www.openscenegraph.org/projects/osg.

[89] Peter S. Pacheco. *Parallel programming with MPI*. Morgan Kaufmann, 1997.

[90] POLKA. http://www.cc.gatech.edu/gvu/softviz/parviz/polka.html.

[91] Blaine A. Price, Ronald M. Baecker and Ian S. Small. A Principled Taxonomy of Software Visualization. *Journal of Visual Languages & Computing*, Volume 4, Number 3, pages 211–266, September 1993.

[92] Blaine A. Price, Ronald M. Baecker and Ian S. Small. An Introduction to software visualization, 1998. MIT Press.

[93] M.J. Quinn. Parallel Programming in C with MPI and OpenMP. *McGraw Hill*, pages 150–154, 2004.

[94] J. Ren, B. Rastegari, A. Condon and H. H. Hoos. HotKnots: heuristic prediction of RNA secondary structures including pseudoknots. *RNA*, Volume 11, Number 10, pages 1494–1504, October 2005.

[95] Guido Rößling. *ANIMAL-FARM: An Extensible Framework for Algorithm Visualization*. Ph.D. thesis, Department of Computer Science and Electronic Engineering, University of Siegen, 2002.

[96] Guido Rößling and B. Freisleben. ANIMAL: A system for supporting multiple roles in algorithm animation. *Journal of Visual Languages and Computing*, Volume 13, Number 3, pages 341–354, 2002.

[97] Guido Rößling and Thomas L. Naps. A testbed for pedagogical requirements in algorithm visualizations. In *ITiCSE '02: Proceedings of the 7th annual conference on Innovation and technology in computer science education*, pages 96–100, New York, NY, USA, 2002. ACM.

[98] Purvi Saraiya, Clifford Shaffer, Scott Mc.Crickard and Chris North. Effective Features of Algorithm Visualizations. *SIGCSE Technical A Symposium on Computer Science Education*, pages 382–386, 2004.

[99] Ghizlane Sbai. Effectiveness and didactical aspects of AV in education (Master's thesis in German). *Department of Computer Science and Mathematics, Goethe Universität Frankfurt/Main*, August 2008.

[100] Georg Schnitger. Algorithmentheorie (In German).
http://www.thi.cs.uni-frankfurt.de/AlgorithmenTheorieWS0809/skript.pdf, pages 32–34.

[101] Georg Schnitger. Parallel Algorithms.
http://www.thi.informatik.uni-frankfurt.de/Parallele/index.html.

[102] Georg Schnitger. Parallel Algorithms.
http://www.thi.informatik.uni-frankfurt.de/Parallele/Parallel05.pdf, 2006.

[103] Georg Schnitger. Data structures (In German). *http://www.thi.cs.uni-frankfurt.de/Datenstrukturen07/skript.pdf*, pages 77–80, 2007.

[104] Georg Schnitger. Data structures (In German). *http://www.thi.cs.uni-frankfurt.de/Datenstrukturen07/skript.pdf*, pages 92–95, 2007.

[105] Georg Schnitger. Algorithmentheorie (In German).
http://www.thi.cs.uni-frankfurt.de/AlgorithmenTheorieWS0809/skript.pdf, pages 50–51, 2009.

[106] Georg Schnitger. Algorithmentheorie (In German).
http://www.thi.cs.uni-frankfurt.de/AlgorithmenTheorieWS0809/skript.pdf, pages 11–11, 2009.

[107] Heidrun Schumann and Wolfgang Müller. *Visualisierung, Grundlagen und allgemeine Methoden (In German)*. Springer, 1999.

[108] Daniel Selman. *Java 3D Programming*. Manning Publications, first edition, 2002.

[109] Clifford A. Shaffer, Matthew Cooper and Stephen H. Edwards. Algorithm visualization: a report on the state of the field. *SIGCSE Bull.*, Volume 39, Number 1, pages 150–154, 2007.

[110] Maria Shneerson and Ayellet Tal. GASP-II: a Geometric Algorithm Animation System for an Electronic Classroom. In *WISDOM Technical Report in Computer Science*, pages 405–406, 1996.

[111] Steven Skiena. The Algorithm Design Manual. page 736. Springer, 2008.

[112] John Stasko. http://gvu.cc.gatech.edu/softviz/algoanim/samba.html.

[113] John Stasko. Tango: A Framework and System for Algorithm Animation. *IEEE Computer*, Volume 23, Number 9, pages 27–39, September 1990.

[114] John Stasko. Animating algorithms with XTANGO. *SIGACT News 23*, pages 7–71, 1992.

[115] John Stasko. Three-Dimensional computation visualization. *IEEE Computer Society Press on Visual Languages*, pages 100–107, 1993.

[116] John Stasko, Albert Badre and Clayton Lewis. Do algorithm animations assist learning?: an empirical study and analysis. In *CHI '93: Proceedings of the INTERACT '93 and CHI '93 conference on Human factors in computing systems*, pages 61–66, New York, NY, USA, 1993. ACM.

[117] SVG. http://svg.org/.

[118] Swing. http://java.sun.com/docs/books/tutorial/uiswing/.

[119] Java 3D Engineering Team. *Java 3D API Tutorial*. Sun Microsystems, http://java.sun.com/developer/onlineTraining/java3d/, 2000.

[120] Java Technology. http://www.sun.com/java/.

[121] Alexander Tillmann, Ashraf Abu Baker and Detlef Krömker. Studienwahl mit Verstand — Mit Self-Assessment Online die Eignung testen (In German). In *Forschung Frankfurt, http://www.forschung-frankfurt.uni-frankfurt.de/2007/Forschung_Frankfurt_2007/3-07/Studienwahl_mit_Verstand__14_.pdf*, pages 70–72, 2007.

[122] Ron Unger and John Moult. Genetic Algorithm for 3D Proteine Folding Simulations. In *Proceedings of the 5th International Conference on Genetic Algorithms*, pages 581–588, San Francisco, CA, USA, 1993. Morgan Kaufmann Publishers Inc.

[123] Algorithm visualisation with Excel. http://www.cs.helsinki.fi/research/aaps/excel/.

[124] Jeffrey Scott Vitter. Design and analysis of dynamic Huffman coding. *Symposium on Foundations of Computer Science*, Volume 0, pages 293–302, 1985.

[125] Overmars von Berg, van Kreveld and Schwarzkopf. *Computational Geometry, Algorithms and Applications*. Springer Verlag, Berlin Heidelberg, 1997.

[126] VPL. http://msdn.microsoft.com/en-us/library/bb483088.aspx.

[127] D. Waston. Keyframe Animation, http://www.cadtutor.net/dd/bryce/anim/anim.html, 1996–2006.

[128] I. Wegener. *Theoretische Informatik. Eine algorithmische Einführung (In German)*. Heidelberg, 2003.

[129] Wikipedia. http://en.wikipedia.org/wiki/Context_menu.

[130] X3D. http://www.web3d.org/x3d/specifications/.

[131] Encodings X3D Specifications and Language Bindings. Internetressource, Nov. 2005.

[132] XML. http://www.w3.org/XML, W3C.

[133] Extensible Markup Language (XML). http://www.w3.org/TR/2006/REC-xml-20060816/, Fourth Edition. Internetressource, Aug. 2006.

Appendix A

Sample Algorithms

A.1 Dijkstra's Algorithm for the SSSP-Problem

Dijkstra is an algorithm that solves the single-source shortest path problem (SSSP-problem) [100, 34] which is defined as follows:

Given a weighted directed Graph G=(V,E) and a weight function $w : E \mapsto \mathbb{R}^+ \cup \{0\}$ which assigns each edge a positive weight ≥ 0. We are looking for the shortest path from a designated source node s to all other nodes of the graph. The weight of a path $p = \langle v_0, v_1, ..., v_k \rangle$ is defined as the sum of the weights of its constituent edges:

$w(p) = \sum_{i=1}^{k} w(v_{i-1}, v_i)$

The **shortest-path weight** from u to v is defined by:

$$delta(u,v) = \begin{cases} min\{w(p) : u \leadsto^p v\} & \text{if there is a path from } u \text{ to } v. \\ \infty & \text{otherwise.} \end{cases}$$

Thus, the **shortest path** from vertex u to vertex v is defined as any path p with a minimal weight.

To solve the SSSP-problem, Dijkstra maintains an initially empty set S of vertices which is gradually filled by vertices whose final shortest-path weights from s have already been computed. Further, the algorithm uses a distance array d of length $|V|$ to save the estimated distances from s to each other node. The algorithm initialises d using the following procedure:

```
INITIALIZE-SINGLE-SOURCE(G, s)
1  for each vertex v ∈ V[G]
2      do d[v] ← ∞
3         π[v] ← NIL
4  d[s] ← 0
```

Listing A.1: Init procedure

As can be seen in the listing, the initially estimated distance from s to itself is zero, and infinite to all other nodes. Π is a predecessor array. For a shortest path p, a node u is a predecessor of v, $if(u,v) \in E$ and (u,v) is an edge in p. Thus, Π includes the subgraph G' which constitutes the shortest path from s to each other node. The algorithm works as follows:

After the initialisation, it repeatedly fetches the node with the minimal estimated distance and moves it from V into S. Whenever a node v is added to S, the algorithm updates the estimated distances to all its adjacent nodes using a technique called relaxation. The following procedure show the implementation of the relax procedure:

```
For each adjacent node v of u
RELAX(u, v, w)
1  if d[v] > d[u] + w(u, v)
2      then d[v] ← d[u] + w(u, v)
3           π[v] ← u
```

Listing A.2: Relax procedure

The algorithm then repeatedly selects the vertex $u \in V \setminus S$ with the minimum shortest-path estimate $(d[u])$, adds u to S, and relaxes all edges leaving u. In the implementation presented by Cormen et al. [34], the algorithm utilises a min-priority queue Q of vertices, keyed by their d values.

```
DIJKSTRA(G, w, s)
1  INITIALIZE-SINGLE-SOURCE(G, s)
2  S ← ∅
3  Q ← V[G]
4  while Q ≠ ∅
5      do u ← EXTRACT-MIN(Q)
6          S ← S ∪ {u}
7          for each vertex v ∈ Adj[u]
8              do RELAX(u, v, w)
```

Listing A.3: Dijkstra's algorithm

As can be seen, S is initially empty, and Q includes all vertices keyed by their d-values. In the first iteration of the *while*-loop, *ExtractMin* returns the start node s. After a node has been added to S, the algorithm fetches all of its adjacent nodes and relaxes them.

Figure 10 shows a screenshot of a simulation of the algorithm. The simulation can also be launched from the following location [2].

A.2 Merge sort

Merge sort is a recursive sorting algorithm that sorts an array $A[0..n]$ as follows:

At the very beginning of the execution, the algorithm computes an index q that partitions A into two subarrays: $A[0..q]$ and $A[q+1..n]$ which contain $\lceil n/2 \rceil$ and $\lfloor n/2 \rfloor$ elements, respectively. The partitioning step is simply repeated until each subarray contains exactly one element. A subarray which contains only one element is already sorted. The algorithm then recursively merges each two sorted subarrays into a new sorted one. To do so, the algorithm copies the elements of the subarrays into two piles (auxiliary arrays) each of which corresponds to one of the subarrays. It then compares the two top elements of the piles, removes the smallest of them and adds it to the output subarray. This merge step is repeated until one of the piles is empty, at which time the remaining input pile is taken and added to the output subarray. The code of merge sort is given as follows:

MERGE-SORT(A, p, r)
1 if $p < r$
2 then $q \leftarrow \lfloor (p+r)/2 \rfloor$
3   MERGE-SORT(A, p, q)
4   MERGE-SORT($A, q+1, r$)
5   MERGE(A, p, q, r)

Listing A.4: Merge sort

MERGE(A, p, q, r)
1 $n_1 \leftarrow q - p + 1$
2 $n_2 \leftarrow r - q$
3 create arrays $L[1 \cdots n_1+1]$ and $R[1 \cdots n_2+1]$ //left and right pile
4 for $i \leftarrow 1$ to n_1
5   do $L[i] \leftarrow A[p+i-1]$
6 for $j \leftarrow 1$ to n_2
7   do $R[j] \leftarrow A[q+j]$
8 $L[n_1+1] \leftarrow \infty$
9 $R[n_2+1] \leftarrow \infty$
10 $i \leftarrow 1$
11 $j \leftarrow 1$
12 for $k \leftarrow p$ to r
13   do if $L[i] \leq R[j]$
14   then $A[k] \leftarrow L[i]$
15          $i \leftarrow i+1$
16   else $A[k] \leftarrow R[j]$
17          $j \leftarrow j+1$

Listing A.5: Merge procedure

Figure 11 shows a screenshot of a simulation of the algorithm. The simulation can be launched from our server at [2].

A.3 Red-Black Trees

A red-black tree [42] is a balanced binary search tree that satisfies the following red-black properties:

1. Every node is either red or black.

2. The root is black.

3. Every leaf (NIL) is black.

4. If a node is red, then both its children are black.

5. For each node, all paths from the node to its descendant leaves contain the same number of black nodes.

We have restricted our introduction of red-black trees to the *delete* operation. Listing A.6 is a simplified pseudo code of this *delete* operation. A more compact version of the code, yet more difficult to understand, can be found in [42].

When a node z is to be deleted, a red-black tree distinguishes between two cases:

Case 1: Both children of z are not nil:

$$left[z] \neq nil[T] \; AND \; right[z] \neq nil[T]$$

In this case the algorithm searches for the successor of z and assigns it to a new variable called y:

$$y \leftarrow TREE - SUCCESSOR(z)$$

146 APPENDIX A. SAMPLE ALGORITHMS

```
Red-Black-Tree-DELETE(T, z)
1   if left[z] ≠ nil[T] AND right[z] ≠ nil[T]   //(case 1)
2       then y ← TREE-SUCCESSOR(z)
3           x ← right[y]
4           p[x] ← p[y]
5           if y = left[p[y]]
6               then left[p[y]] ← x
7               else right[p[y]] ← x
8
9           key[z] ← key[y]
10          if color[y] = BLACK
11              then RB-DELETE-FIXUP(T, x)
12
13  else  //left[z] = nil[T] OR right[z] = nil[T] (case 2)
14      if left[z] ≠ nil[T]
15          then x ← left[z]
16          else x ← right[z]
17      p[x] ← p[z]
18      if p[z] = nil[T]
19          then root[T] ← x
20          else if z = left[p[z]]
21              then left[p[z]] ← x
22              else right[p[z]] ← x
23      if color[z] = BLACK
24          then RB-DELETE-FIXUP(T, x)
```

Listing A.6: Delete operation of a red-black tree

The successor [31] of a node z in a binary search tree is the node with the smallest key greater than $key[z]$. Let x be the right child of y ($x \leftarrow right[y]$) and p the parent of the successor ($p = p[y]$). If the successor of z is the left child of its parent then x is attached to p as its left child, otherwise x is attached to p as its right child. In both cases p becomes the parent of x: $x \leftarrow right[y]$
$p[x] \leftarrow p[y]$
$if\ y\ =\ left[p[y]]$
$\quad then\ left[p[y]] \leftarrow x$
$\quad else\ right[p[y]] \leftarrow x$

Next, the algorithm overwrites the key of z by the key of the successor. Finally, if the successor is a black node, the algorithm performs a $delete - fixup$ operation (see below) starting at node x:

A.3. RED-BLACK TREES

$key[z] \leftarrow key[y]$

$if\ color[y]\ =\ BLACK$

$\quad then\ RB - DELETE - FIXUP(T, x)$

Case 2: At least one of the children of z is nil:

$$left[z]\ =\ nil[T]\ OR\ right[z]\ =\ nil[T]$$

In this case, if the left child of z ($left[z]$) is not nil, x is assigned $left[z]$ otherwise x is assigned $right[z]$:

$if\ left[z]\ \neq nil[T]$

$\quad then\ x \leftarrow left[z]$

$\quad else\ x \leftarrow right[z])$

Note that x will point to nil if both children of z are nil. If z is the root of the tree, then it is replaced by x, otherwise x is attached to the parent of z either as its left or its right child. This depends on whether z is the left or the right child of its parent:

$p[x] \leftarrow p[z]$

$\quad if\ p[z]\ =\ nil[T]$

$\quad\quad then\ root[T]\ \leftarrow x$

$\quad\quad else\ if\ z\ =\ left[p[z]]$

$\quad\quad\quad then\ left[p[z]] \leftarrow x$

$\quad\quad\quad else\ right[p[z]] \leftarrow x$

Finally, if z is a black node, the algorithm will launch a **delete-fixup** procedure:

$if\ color[z] = BLACK$

$\quad then\ RB - DELETE - FIXUP(T, x)$

As the *delete* operation is likely to transform the tree into a tree that does not satisfy all red-black priorities above, the red-black tree invokes the RB-DELETE-FIXUP(T, x) routine to restore any violated properties. Listing A.7 shows the code of the operation.

```
Red-Black-Tree-DELETE-FIXUP(T, x)
1  while x ≠ root[T] and color[x] = BLACK
2    do if x = left[p[x]]
3       then w ← right[p[x]]
4            if color[w] = RED
5               then color[w] ← BLACK
6                    color[p[x]] ← RED
7                    LEFT-ROTATE(T, p[x])
8                    w ← right[p[x]]
9            if color[left[w]] = BLACK and color[right[w]] = BLACK
10              then color[w] ← RED
11                   x ← p[x]
12           else if color[right[w]] = BLACK
13                  then color[left[w]] ← BLACK
14                       color[w] ← RED
15                       RIGHT-ROTATE(T, w)
16                       w ← right[p[x]]
17                color[w] ← color[p[x]]
18                color[p[x]] ← BLACK
19                color[right[w]] ← BLACK
20                LEFT-ROTATE(T, p[x])
21                x ← root[T]
22     else (same as then clause with "right" and "left" exchanged)
23 color[x] ← BLACK
```

Listing A.7: Delete-Fixup operation of a red-black tree

The routine restores any violated properties by recolouring some nodes and performing two rotation operations: **left-rotate** and **right-rotate**. The details of both operations are given in [42].

Figure 8 shows a simulation of a red-black tree. The simulation can also be launched from our server located at [2].

Appendix B

Source Code Listings

B.1 Augmented Code Example

Augmented Code Example

```
/*~
 * @expandableBlock start
 */
@highlight
public BinaryNode delete(Integer key) {
    /*~
     * @narrative deleting $key ...
     * @controlPoint delay
     */
    BinaryNode z = lookupRec(key);
    if (z != null) {
        /*~
         * @narrative $key deleted!
         * @controlPoint stop
         * @snapshot
         */
        return delete(z);
    }
```

```
            else{
                        /*~
                         * @narrative $key does not exist!
                         * @controlPoint stop
                         * @snapshot
                         */
                        return null;
            }
}
/*~
 * @expandableBlock end
 */
/*~
 * @expandableBlock start
 */
@highlight
private BinaryNode delete(BinaryNode z) {
            BinaryNode y = null;
            BinaryNode x = null;
            if (z.leftChild == null || z.rightChild == null)
                        y = z;
            else
                        y = successor(z);
            if (y.leftChild != null)
                        x = y.leftChild;
            else
                        x = y.rightChild;
            if (x != null)
                        /*~
                         * @controlPoint delay
                         */
                        x.setParent(y.getParent());
            if (y.getParent() == null)
                        /*~
                         * @controlPoint delay
                         */
```

B.1. AUGMENTED CODE EXAMPLE

```
            setRoot(x);
        else if (y == y.getParent().leftChild)
            /*~
             * @controlPoint delay
             */
            y.getParent().setLeftChild(x);
        else
            /*~
             * @controlPoint delay
             */
            y.getParent().setRightChild(x);
        if (y != z)
            z.setKey(y.key);
        /*~
         * @controlPoint stop
         * @snapshot
         */
        return y;
    }
    /*~
     * @expandableBlock end
     */
```

Listing B.1: An augmented code of the delete operation of a binary search tree

B.2 Python Scanner

```java
/**
 * 3D-VISIAN-Project http://www.3dvisian.de
 * @3DVISIAN (#) visian3d.api.utilities.PythonScanner.java
 * Created on 02.02.2008
 * Copyright (c) 2007-2009, Inc. All Rights Reserved.
 * Goethe-Universität Frankfurt/Main, Department of Computer Science and Mathematics,
 * Institute of Computer Graphics (Prof. Dr. Detlef Krömker)
 * http://www.gdv.informatik.uni-frankfurt.de
 *
 * @author Ashraf Abu Baker
 * @version 1.0
 */
package visian3d.api.scanner;

import java.io.IOException;
import java.io.InputStream;
import java.net.URL;
import java.util.HashMap;
import java.util.Map;

public class PythonScanner extends Scanner {
    public static final int FUNCTION = 11;
    public static final int SELF = 12;
    public static final int NONE_TRUE_FALSE=13;
    public static final String languageVersionSupported = "Python 2.6";
```

B.2. PYTHON SCANNER

```java
private static final String[] keywords = { "and","as", "assert", "break",
                "class", "continue", "def", "del", "elif", "else", "except","False",
                "exec", "finally", "for", "from", "global", "if", "import", "in",
                "is", "lambda", "not", "or", "pass", "print", "raise", "return",
                "True","try", "while", "with", "yield", "None" };
static final Map<String, Integer> keywordIndex;

private StringBuilder buffer = new StringBuilder();

private boolean functionMode=false;

static {
        keywordIndex = new HashMap<String, Integer>();
        for (int i = 0; i < keywords.length; i++) {
                keywordIndex.put(keywords[i], i);
        }
}

        public PythonScanner(URL url) throws IOException {
                super(url);
        }
        public PythonScanner(InputStream is) throws IOException {
                super(is);
        }
        public PythonScanner(String doc) {
                super(doc);
        }

@Override
/**
 * Returns the next lexical token in the document.
 */
public int nextToken() {
        int c;
        this.currentTockenStartIndex = this.currentCharIndex;
        while (true) {

                switch (c = read()) {
                case END_OF_FILE:
                        return END_OF_FILE;
                case '#': // line comment
                        unread(c);
                        while (true) {
                                c = read();
                                if ((c == END_OF_FILE) || (c == END_OF_LINE)) {
                                        // unread(c);
                                        return LINE_COMMENT;
                                }
                        }

                case '"': // comment or string
                        c = read();
                        if (c == '"') {// either comment or empty string
                                c = read();
                                if (c != '"')// empty comment
                                        return STRING;
                                for (;;) {// three " (""") has been read
```

```java
                        c = read();
                        switch (c) {
                        case '"'://first '"' in end of empty comment found
                                c = read();
                                if (c == '"') {// probably empty comment
                                        c = read();
                                        if (c == '"')
                                        return MULTILINE_COMMENT;
                                }
                                return UNSUPPORTED_TOKEN;
                        case END_OF_FILE:

                                return UNSUPPORTED_TOKEN;
                        case '\\':
                                c = read();
                                if(c==END_OF_FILE)
                                        return UNSUPPORTED_TOKEN;
                                break;
                        }
                }
        }
        else if(c==END_OF_FILE)
                return UNSUPPORTED_TOKEN;
        //its a string
        for (;;) {
                c = read();
                switch (c) {
                case '"':
                        return STRING;// string
                case END_OF_FILE:
                        // unread(c);
                        return UNSUPPORTED_TOKEN;
                case '\\':
                        c = read();
                        if(c==END_OF_FILE)
                                return UNSUPPORTED_TOKEN;
                        c = read();
                        break;
                }
        }
case '0':               case '1':               case '2':
case '3':               case '4':               case '5':
case '6':               case '7':               case '8':
case '9':
        do {
                c = read();
        } while (Character.isDigit((char) c) || c == 'x' || c == 'X');
        // Hexdecimal,decimal and octal numbers
                unread(c);
        return NUMBER;
default:
        if (Character.isWhitespace((char) c)) {
                do {                                                    c = read();
                } while (Character.isWhitespace((char) c));
                unread(c);
                // return WHITESPACE;
                return UNSUPPORTED_TOKEN;
```

B.2. PYTHON SCANNER 155

```
                            }
                            if (isPythonIdentifierStart((char) c)) {
                                    buffer.setLength(0);
                                    do {
                                            buffer.append((char) c);
                                            c = read();
                                    } while (isPythonIdetifierPart((char) c));
                                    unread(c);
                                    Integer i = keywordIndex.get(buffer.toString());
                                    if (i != null) {
                                            String keyword=buffer.toString();
              if(keyword.equals("None")||keyword.equals("False")||keyword.equals("False"))
                                                    return NONE_TRUE_FALSE;
                                            else
              if(keyword.equals("class")||keyword.equals("def"))
                                                    this.functionMode=true;
                                                    return KEYWORD;
                                    }
                                    if(buffer.toString().equals("self"))
                                            return SELF;
                                    // return WORD;
                                    if(functionMode){
                                            functionMode=false;
                                            return FUNCTION;
                                    }
                                    return UNSUPPORTED_TOKEN;
                            }
                            // return OTHER;
                            return UNSUPPORTED_TOKEN;
                    }
            }
    }
    private boolean isPythonIdentifierStart(char c){
            switch(c){
            case '_':
            case 'e':        case 'a':        case 'b':        case 'c':        case 'd':
            case 'j': case 'k':    case 'f':        case 'g':        case 'h':        case 'i':
            case 'o':                    case 'l': case 'm':        case 'n':
            case 't': case 'u':   case 'p':        case 'q':        case 'r': case 's':
            case 'y':                       case 'v':        case 'w':        case 'x':
            case 'D':        case 'z':        case 'A':        case 'B':        case 'C':
            case 'I': case 'J':  case 'E':        case 'F':        case 'G':        case 'H':
            case 'N':        case 'O':   case 'K':        case 'L':        case 'M':
            case 'S':        case 'T':        case 'P':        case 'Q':        case 'R':
            case 'X':        case 'Y':        case 'U':        case 'V':        case 'W':
            default:return  false;             case 'Z':return true;
            }
    }
    private boolean isPythonIdetifierPart(char c){
            return (isPythonIdentifierStart(c)||Character.isDigit(c));
    }
}
```

```
            while (children.hasMoreElements()) {
                    Node childNode = children.nextElement();
                    if (childNode instanceof IUndoableNode)

                            if (childNode instanceof IUndoableGroup)
                                    reconstructUGroup((IUndoableGroup) childNode);
                            else
                                    reconstructUNode((IUndoableNode) childNode);
                    else if (childNode instanceof Group)
                            reconstructGroup((Group) childNode);
                    else
                            reconstructNode(childNode);

            }
    }

    private void reconstructUNode(IUndoableNode node) {
            node.restoreSnapshot(snapshotID);
    }

    private void reconstructNode(Node node) {
            if (node instanceof Shape3D) {
                    Shape3D shape = (Shape3D) node;
                    Appearance app = shape.getAppearance();
                    if (app instanceof IUndoableObject)
                            ((IUndoableObject) app).restoreSnapshot(snapshotID);
                    Geometry geom = shape.getGeometry();
                    Shape3D shape = (Shape3D) node;
                    Appearance app = shape.getAppearance();
                    if (app instanceof IUndoableObject)
                            ((IUndoableObject) app).restoreSnapshot(snapshotID);
                    Geometry geom = shape.getGeometry();
                    if (geom instanceof IUndoableObject)
                            ((IUndoableObject) geom).restoreSnapshot(snapshotID);
            }
    }

    private void reconstructUGroup(IUndoableGroup uGroup) {

            uGroup.restoreSnapshot(snapshotID);
            uGroup.removeAllChildren();
            int uGroupKey = uGroup.getHashKey();

            LinkedHashMap<Integer, Integer> children = keys.get(uGroupKey);

            if (children == null) {

                    return;
            }

            for (Integer child : children.keySet()) {
                    Integer childType = children.get(child);

                    switch (childType) {
```

B.3 Visual Merge sort

Visual Mergesort Simulation

```
/**
 * 3D-VISIAN-Project http://www.3dvisian.de
 * @3DVISIAN (#)visian3d.visualsimulation.sortingalgorithms.VisualMergeSort.java
 * Created on 05.10.2008
 * Copyright (c) 2007-2009, Inc. All Rights Reserved.
 * Goethe-Universität Frankfurt/Main, Department of Computer Science and Mathematics,
 * Institute of Computer Graphics (Prof. Dr. Detlef Krömker)
 * http://www.gdv.informatik.uni-frankfurt.de
 *
 * @author Ashraf Abu Baker
 * @version 1.0
 */
package visian3d.visualsimulation.sortingalgorithms;

import javax.vecmath.Vector3d;
import javax.vecmath.Vector3f;
import visian3d.api.ui.SimulationContext;
import visian3d.visualsimulation.datastructures.arrays.VisualArray;
import visian3d.visualsimulation.datastructures.arrays.VisualArraySimulation;
```

```java
public class VisualMergeSort extends VisualArraySimulation {

    private HashMap<Integer, String> mapping = new HashMap<Integer, String>();
    private int callNumber = 0;

    @Override
    public void start() {

        super.start();

        settingPanel.setInputArray(ArrayGen.createRandomArray(8, 8));
        if (!readInput())
            return;
        callNumber = 0;
        VisualArray A = new VisualArray(as.inputArray, as, as.translation);
        A.addNumber(callNumber++);
        this.showArray(A, 0, A.length - 1);
        as.translation.y = as.translation.y - as.y_translation;
        Vector3f position = A.getAbsolutePosition();
        position.y = position.y - as.y_translation;
        mergeSort(A.getSubArray(0, A.length - 1, position), 0, A.length - 1);
        this.finished();

    }

    public void mergeSort(VisualArray A, int left, int right)

    {
        A.addNumber(callNumber++);
        this.showArray(A, left, right);
        if (left < right) {
            int middle = (right + left) / 2;

            Vector3f translation1 = getStartPosition(left, middle, right, A
                            .getAbsolutePosition());
            VisualArray B = A.getSubArray(left, middle, translation1);

            mergeSort(B, 0, B.length - 1);
            int i, j;

            for (i = 0; i < B.length; i++)
                A.assign(i, B.getFieldSR(i));
```

B.3. VISUAL MERGE SORT

```
            Vector3f translation2 = getStartPosition2(left, middle, right,
                        translation1.x, A.getAbsolutePosition());

            VisualArray C = A.getSubArray(middle + 1, right, translation2);

            mergeSort(C, 0, C.length - 1);
            j = i;

            for (i = 0; i < C.length; i++)
                    A.assign(j++, C.getFieldSR(i));

            setBreakpoint();

            B.addLeftArrow();

            C.addRightArrow();

            merge(A, left, middle, right, B, C);
            B.unhighlightArrows();
            C.unhighlightArrows();
        }
    }

    private Vector3f getStartPosition2(int p, int q, int r,
                float starPoistion1X, Vector3f position) {
        int L1 = q - p + 1;
        int L2 = r - q;

        float innerGab = L1 * as.fieldWidth + Math.min(L1, L2) * as.fieldWidth
                / 2;
        return new Vector3f(position.x + innerGab, position.y
                    - as.y_translation, position.z);
    }

    private Vector3f getStartPosition(int p, int q, int r, Vector3f position) {

        int L1 = q - p + 1;
        int L2 = r - q;
        float leftTranslation = Math.min(L1, L2) * as.fieldWidth / 2;
        Vector3f translation1 = new Vector3f(position.x - leftTranslation,
                    position.y - as.y_translation, position.z);
        return translation1;
    }

    private void showArray(VisualArray A, int p, int r) {

        if (!(r >= p))
                return;
        this.visManager.addChild(A);
        this.setBreakpointAndTakeSnapshot();
```

```
}

public void merge(VisualArray A, int left, int middle, int right,
                VisualArray B, VisualArray C) {

    int n1 = middle - left + 1;
    int n2 = right - middle;
    VisualArray L = new VisualArray(n1 + 1, as, mapping, new Vector3f(
                as.translation.x - as.fieldWidth * (middle - left + 1 + 1),
                as.translation.y + 2 * as.y_translation, 0));
    VisualArray R = new VisualArray(n2 + 1, as, mapping, new Vector3f(
                as.translation.x + as.fieldWidth * (right - middle + 1),
                as.translation.y + 2 * as.y_translation, 0));

    A.markSubArray(0, A.length - 1);

    L.setValue(L.length - 1, Integer.MAX_VALUE);
    R.setValue(R.length - 1, Integer.MAX_VALUE);
    this.showArray(L, 0, L.length - 1);
    this.showArray(R, 0, R.length - 1);
    int i = 0;

    for (i = 0; i < L.length - 1; i++) {

            L.assignAn(i, B.getField(i));
            this.setBreakpoint();
            ;
    }

    int j = 0;
    for (j = 0; j < R.length - 1; j++) {
            R.assignAn(j, C.getField(j));
            this.setBreakpoint();

    }

    i = 0;
    j = 0;
    this.takeSnapshot();

    for (int k = left; k <= right; k++) {

            if (L.getFieldS(i).compareTo(R.getFieldS(j)) <= 0) {

                    A.assignAn(A.getFieldSR(k), L.getField(i));
                    i++;
                    setBreakpoint();
```

B.3. VISUAL MERGE SORT

```
                } else {
                        A.assignAn(A.getFieldSR(k), R.getField(j));
                        j++;
                }
                this.setBreakpointAndTakeSnapshot();
        }
        L.detach();
        R.detach();
        A.removeMarker();
}

@Override
public void init(SimulationContext sc) {
        super.init(sc);
        try {
                setSourceCodes(this.getClass(), new VisualMergeSort_Mapping());
                narrativeSettingDocInfTabbedPane.addTab("Quiz", new ImageIcon(
                        ResourceGetter.getResource(this.getClass(),
                        "images/quiz3.png")), new ScrollableTextPane(),
                        "Quiz");
        } catch (Exception e) {
                e.printStackTrace();
        }

        sc.setTitle("MergeSort");
        this.setDefaultCameraPosition(new Vector3d(0, 0.1, 5));
        this.resetCamera();
        mapping.put(Integer.MAX_VALUE, "∞");
        try {
                setSourceCodes(this.getClass(), new VisualMergeSort_Mapping());
        } catch (Exception e) {
                e.printStackTrace();
        }

        sc.setCodeTabbedPane(codeManager);
    }
}
```

Listing B.3: Visual merge sort

B.4 Visian Comment Parser

Visian Comment Parser

```java
/**
 * 3D-VISIAN-Project http://www.3dvisian.de
 * @3DVISIAN  visian3d.codegenerator.VisianCommentParser.java
 * Created on 17.11.2007
 * Copyright (c) 2007-2009, Inc. All Rights Reserved.
 * Goethe-Universität Frankfurt/Main, Department of Computer Science and Mathematics,
 * Institute of Computer Graphics (Prof. Dr. Detlef Krömker)
 * http://www.gdv.informatik.uni-frankfurt.de
 *
 * @author Ashraf Abu Baker
 * @version 1.0
 */
package visian3d.codegenerator;

import static visian3d.codegenerator.utilities.Utilities.*;
import java.util.*;
import org.eclipse.jdt.core.dom.*;
import visian3d.api.code.CodePointLabel;
import visian3d.codegenerator.utilities.Utilities;

public class VisianCommentParser {
    public static String INTERNAL_METHOD_INVOCATION = "INTERNAL_METHOD_INVOCATION";
    private OwnerSetter os;
    private CompilationUnit unit;
    public SortedMap<Integer, CodePointLabel.Point> lPoints;
    public ArrayList<VisianComment> visianComments;
    public VisianCommentParser(CompilationUnit unit) {
        this.unit = unit;

        parseVisianCommentList();
    }
```

```java
        public HashMap<Integer, Integer> getStartAndEndLineNrOfMethods() {
            return os.getStartAndEndLineNrOfMethods();
        }

        public void parseVisianCommentList() {
            visianComments = new ArrayList<VisianComment>();
            List<Comment> comments = unit.getCommentList();
            int i = 0;
            Javadoc javadoc = null;

            for (Comment comment : comments) {

                if (!comment.isDocComment())
                    continue;
                javadoc = (Javadoc) comment;
                if (!isVisianDocComment(javadoc, unit))
                    continue;

                visianComments.add(new VisianComment(javadoc, unit, i++,
                                    getLineNumberAtEnd(unit, javadoc)));

            }
            computeControlPoints();

            setOwners();
        }
        public void computeControlPoints() {
            controllPoints = new TreeMap<Integer, CodePointLabel.Point>();
            for (VisianComment visianComment : visianComments) {
                if (visianComment.containsTag(VisianComment.DELAY_TAG)) {
                    controllPoints.put(visianComment.endLineNumber,
                                    CodePointLabel.Point.DELAY_POINT);
                    visianComment.javadocComment.setProperty(VisianComment.BD,
                                    VisianComment.DELAY_TAG);
                } else if (visianComment.containsTag(VisianComment.BREAK_TAG)) {
                    controllPoints.put(visianComment.endLineNumber,
                                    CodePointLabel.Point.BREAK_POINT);
                    visianComment.javadocComment.setProperty(VisianComment.BD,
                                    VisianComment.BREAK_TAG);
                }
            }
        }

        private void setOwners() {
            os = new OwnerSetter(visianComments);
            unit.accept(os);
        }

        public ArrayList<VisianComment> getVisianCommentList() {

            return visianComments;
        }
```

```java
        public SortedMap<Integer, CodePointLabel.Point> getIPoints() {
            return IPoints;
        }

        public static boolean isVisianDocComment(Javadoc comment,
                            CompilationUnit unit) {
            return (comment.isDocComment()
                        && comment.tags().size() > 0
                        && (((TagElement) comment.tags().get(0))).fragments().get(0)
                .toString().startsWith("~") && unit
                .getLineNumber(comment.getStartPosition()) == unit
.getLineNumber(((ASTNode) (((TagElement) comment.tags().get(0)))
                                        .fragments().get(0)).getStartPosition()));

        }
        public static boolean isStartLineOfVisianMultilineComment(String line) {
            return (line

        .startsWith(CommentRecognizer.VISIAN_MULTILINE_COMMENT_START));

        }
public static boolean isStartLineOfJavaMultilineComment(String line) {
            return
(line.startsWith(CommentRecognizer.JAVA_MULTILINE_COMMENT_START));

        }
        public static boolean containsEndOfVisianMultilineComment(String line) {
            return line.indexOf(CommentRecognizer.VISIAN_MULTILINE_COMMENT_END)
                            != -1;
        }

}


class OwnerSetter extends ASTVisitor {

        ArrayList<VisianComment> comments;
        CompilationUnit unit;
        List<String> internalMethods = new ArrayList<String>();
        List<String> classNames = new ArrayList<String>();
        private HashMap<Integer, Integer> startAndEndLineNrOfMethods = new
        HashMap<Integer, Integer>();


        public OwnerSetter(ArrayList<VisianComment> comments) {
            this.comments = comments;
        }

        public HashMap<Integer, Integer> getStartAndEndLineNrOfMethods() {
            return this.startAndEndLineNrOfMethods;
        }
```

B.4. VISIAN COMMENT PARSER

```java
@Override
public boolean visit(CompilationUnit unit) {
    List list = unit.types();
    this.unit = unit;
    this.findInternalMethods();

    return true;
}

private void findInternalMethods() {
    List<BodyDeclaration> types = unit.types();

    boolean found = false;
    for (BodyDeclaration type : types) {

        if (type instanceof TypeDeclaration) {
            TypeDeclaration td = (TypeDeclaration) type;

    if (!td.isInterface()) {
      List<IExtendedModifier> modifiers = td.modifiers();
      for (IExtendedModifier modAnn : modifiers) {
            if (modAnn.isAnnotation()) {
                Annotation ann = (Annotation) modAnn;

                if (ann.getTypeName().toString().equals(
                                        Annotations.HighlightMethods)) {
    this.setInternalMethods(td);
    found = true;

            }

        } else {
            Modifier mod = (Modifier) modAnn;
            if (mod.isPublic()) {
                this.setInternalMethods(td);
                found = true;
                            }
                        }
                    }
                }
            }

    }
    if (!found && types.size() > 0) {
        BodyDeclaration type = types.get(0);
        if (type != null) {
            if (type instanceof TypeDeclaration) {
                TypeDeclaration td = (TypeDeclaration) type;
                if (!td.isInterface()) {
                    this.setInternalMethods(td);
                    return;
                }
```

```java
                        }
                    }
                }
            }
        }
    }

    private void setInternalMethods(TypeDeclaration td) {

        MethodDeclaration[] methods = td.getMethods();

        for (MethodDeclaration method : methods) {
            List paramters = method.parameters();
            internalMethods.add(method.parameters().size() + "#"
                    + method.getName().toString());
        }

    }

    @Override
    public void endVisit(CompilationUnit unit) {

        assignCommentsToOwnerAndMarkPauseTagStatments();

    }

    private void assignCommentsToOwnerAndMarkPauseTagStatments() {
        for (VisianComment comment : comments) {

            Object commentList = comment.owner
                    .getProperty(VisianComment.VISIAN_COMMENT);

            if (commentList == null) {
                ArrayList<VisianComment> newCommentList = new
                ArrayList<VisianComment>();
                newCommentList.add(comment);

comment.owner.setProperty(VisianComment.VISIAN_COMMENT,
                        newCommentList);
            } else {

                ((ArrayList<VisianComment>) commentList).add(comment);
            }

            if ((comment.containsTag(VisianComment.DELAY_TAG) || comment
                    .containsTag(VisianComment.BREAK_TAG))
                    && comment.owner.getNodeType() ==
                    ASTNode.BLOCK) {

                Block block = (Block) comment.owner;
                int endLineOfComment = getLineNumberAtEnd(unit,
                        comment.javadocComment);
                List<Statement> statements = block.statements();
```

B.4. VISIAN COMMENT PARSER

```java
                        boolean found = false;
                        for (Statement st : statements) {
                                if (Utilities.getLineNumberAtStart(unit, st) >
                                   endLineOfComment) {
                                        st.setProperty(VisianComment.BD, comment);
                                        found = true;
                                        break;
                                }
                        }
                        if (!found) {
                                block.setProperty(VisianComment.BD, comment);
                        }
                }
            }
        }
    }

    @Override
    public boolean visit(Block block) {
        updateOwner(block);
        return true;
    }
    private boolean isInternalMethod(MethodInvocation method) {
        if (internalMethods
                    .contains(((method.arguments()).size() + "#" + method.getName()
                                .toString())))
                return true;

        return false;
    }

    @Override
    public boolean visit(ClassInstanceCreation cic) {
        Type type = cic.getType();
        String name = "";
        while (!(type instanceof SimpleType))
                type = ((ParameterizedType) type).getType();
        name = ((SimpleType) type).getName().toString();
        if (!this.internalMethods.contains(cic.typeArguments().size() + "#"
                    + name))
                return true;
        ASTNode parent = cic.getParent();
        while (parent != null) {
                if (parent instanceof Statement) {
```

```java
                    if (Utilities.ignorMetodInvocation((Statement) parent)) {
                        return true;
                    }
                    parent.setProperty(

                    VisianCommentParser.INTERNAL_METHOD_INVOCATION,
                    Utilities.getLineNumberAtStart(unit, parent));

                    return true;
                }

                parent = parent.getParent();
            }
            System.out.println();
            return true;
        }

        @Override
        public boolean visit(MethodDeclaration method) {

            if (internalMethods
                    .contains(((method.modifiers()).size() + "#" + method.getName()
                            .toString()))) {

                this.startAndEndLineNrOfMethods.put(unit.getLineNumber(method
                        .getStartPosition()), unit.getLineNumber(method
                        .getStartPosition()
                        + method.getLength() - 1));
            }
            return true;
        }

        @Override
        public boolean visit(MethodInvocation method) {

            if (!isInternalMethod(method))
                return true;

            ASTNode parent = method.getParent();
            while (parent != null) {
                if (parent instanceof Statement) {

                    if (Utilities.ignorMetodInvocation((Statement) parent)) {

                        return true;
                    }

                    parent.setProperty(

                    VisianCommentParser.INTERNAL_METHOD_INVOCATION,
                    Utilities.getLineNumberAtStart(unit, parent));
```

B.4. VISIAN COMMENT PARSER

```java
                    return true;
                }
                
                parent = parent.getParent();
            }
            System.out.println();
            return true;
        }
        
        @Override
        public boolean visit(ForStatement _for) {
            
            if (isSingleStatementFor(_for)) {
                System.out.println("foor");
                updateOwner2(_for);
            }
            
            return true;
        }
        
        @Override
        public boolean visit(EnhancedForStatement _for) {
            
            if (isSingleStatementEnhancedFor(_for)) {
                System.out.println("_foor");
                updateOwner2(_for);
            }
            return true;
        }
        
        @Override
        public boolean visit(WhileStatement _while) {
            
            if (isSingleStatementWhile(_while))
                updateOwner2(_while);
            return true;
        }
        
        @Override
        public boolean visit(DoStatement _do) {
            
            if (isSingleStatementDo(_do)) {
                System.out.println("do");
                updateOwner2(_do);
            }
            return true;
        }
```

```java
@Override
public boolean visit(IfStatement _if) {

    if (isSingleStatementThen(_if))
        updateOwner2(_if);

    if (isSingleStatementElse(_if))
        updateOwner2(_if);
    return true;
}

@Override
public boolean visit(TypeDeclaration td) {

    updateOwner(td);
    return true;
}

private void updateOwner(ASTNode owner) {

    int start = owner.getStartPosition();
    int end = start + owner.getLength() - 1;
    int commentStart;
    int commentEnd;
    int ownerStart;
    int ownerEnd;
    for (VisianComment comment : comments) {
        commentStart = comment.javadocComment.getStartPosition();
        commentEnd = commentStart + comment.javadocComment.getLength() - 1;
        if (commentStart > start && commentEnd < end) {
            ownerStart = comment.owner.getStartPosition();
            ownerEnd = ownerStart + comment.owner.getLength() - 1;
            if (start > ownerStart && end < ownerEnd)
                comment.owner = owner;
        }
    }
}

private void updateOwner2(ASTNode potentialOwner) {

    int potetnialOwnerStart = potentialOwner.getStartPosition();
    int commentStart;
    int commentEnd;
    for (VisianComment comment : comments) {
        if (!comment.containsTag(VisianComment.DELAY_TAG)
                &&
                !comment.containsTag(VisianComment.BREAK_TAG))
            continue;

        commentStart = comment.javadocComment.getStartPosition();
        commentEnd = commentStart + comment.javadocComment.getLength() - 1;
```

B.4. VISIAN COMMENT PARSER

```java
            if (potentialOwner instanceof ForStatement){
                ForStatement _for = (ForStatement) potentialOwner;
                if (isSingleStatementFor(_for)){
                    int singelStatmentStart = _for.getBody().getStartPosition();
                    if (commentStart > potetnialOwnerStart
                            && commentEnd < singelStatmentStart){

_for.getBody().setProperty(VisianComment.BD,
                                                            comment);
                                        comment.owner = _for;
                                        continue;
                    }
                }
            }
            if (potentialOwner instanceof EnhancedForStatement){
                EnhancedForStatement _for = (EnhancedForStatement)
                    potentialOwner;
                if (isSingleStatementEnhancedFor(_for)){
                    int singelStatmentStart = _for.getBody().getStartPosition();
                    if (commentStart > potetnialOwnerStart
                        && commentEnd < singelStatmentStart){

_for.getBody().setProperty(VisianComment.BD,
                                                            comment);
                                        comment.owner = _for;
                                        continue;
                    }
                }
            }
            if (potentialOwner instanceof DoStatement){
                DoStatement _do = (DoStatement) potentialOwner;
                if (isSingleStatementDo(_do)){
                    int singelStatmentStart =
                            _do.getBody().getStartPosition();
                    if (commentStart > potetnialOwnerStart
                            && commentEnd <
                                    singelStatmentStart){

_do.getBody().setProperty(VisianComment.BD,
                                                            comment);
                                        comment.owner = _do;
                                        continue;
                    }
                }
            }
            if (potentialOwner instanceof WhileStatement){
                WhileStatement _while = (WhileStatement) potentialOwner;
                if (isSingleStatementWhile(_while)){
                    int singelStatmentStart = _while.getBody()
                            .getStartPosition();
```

```
                            if (commentStart > potetnialOwnerStart
                                    && commentEnd < singelStatmentStart) {

                                _while.getBody().setProperty(VisianComment.BD, comment);
                                ;
                                comment.owner = _while;
                                continue;
                            }
                        }
                    }
                    if (potentialOwner instanceof IfStatement) {
                        IfStatement _if = (IfStatement) potentialOwner;
                        if (isSingleStatementThen(_if)) {
                            int singelStatmentStart = _if.getThenStatement()
                                    .getStartPosition();
                            if (commentStart > potetnialOwnerStart
                                    && commentEnd <
singelStatmentStart) {

                                _if.getThenStatement().setProperty(VisianComment.BD,
                                            comment);
                                comment.owner = _if;

                            }
                        }
                        if (isSingleStatementElse(_if)) {
                            int singelStatmentStart = _if.getElseStatement()
                                    .getStartPosition();
                            if (commentStart > potetnialOwnerStart
                                    && commentEnd <
                                    singelStatmentStart) {

                                _if.getElseStatement().setProperty(VisianComment.BD,

                                        comment);
                                comment.owner = _if;
                            }
                        }
                    }
                }
            }
        }
    }
}
```

Listing B.4: Visian comment parser

B.5 Visual Array

Visual Array

package visian3d.visualsimulation.datastructures.arrays;

import java.util.*;
import javax.vecmath.*;
import javax.media.j3d.Alpha;
import javax.media.j3d.BoundingSphere;
import javax.media.j3d.BranchGroup;
import javax.media.j3d.Group;
import javax.media.j3d.Node;
import javax.media.j3d.PositionPathInterpolator;
import javax.media.j3d.Text3D;
import javax.media.j3d.Transform3D;
import javax.media.j3d.TransformGroup;
import visian3d.api.utilities.Navigator;
import visian3d.api.utilities.UndoableObjectsFactory;
import visian3d.undo.j3d.ComparableColor3f;
import visian3d.undo.j3d.ComparableTransform3D;
import visian3d.undo.j3d.UndoableBranchGroup;
import visian3d.undo.j3d.UndoableTransformGroup;
import visian3d.visualsimulation.utilities.Arrow;
import visian3d.visualsimulation.utilities.SharedNodeComponents;

```java
public class VisualArray extends UndoableBranchGroup {

    public ArrayField<Integer>[] fields;
    public ArraySimulationSetting as;
    public UndoableTransformGroup rootTG;
    PPI ppi;
    public int length;
    private UndoableBranchGroup markerTG;
    public HashMap<Integer, String> mapping;

    public VisualArray(int size, ArraySimulationSetting as) {
        this(size, as, Text3D.ALIGN_CENTER, null);
    }
    public VisualArray(int size, ArraySimulationSetting as,
                HashMap<Integer, String> mapping) {
        this(size, as, Text3D.ALIGN_CENTER, mapping);
    }

    public VisualArray(int size, ArraySimulationSetting as,
                HashMap<Integer, String> mapping, Vector3f translation) {
        this(size, as, Text3D.ALIGN_CENTER, mapping, translation);
    }

    public VisualArray(int size, Vector3f absolutePosition,
                ArraySimulationSetting as) {
        Integer[] input = new Integer[size];
        for (int i = 0; i < size; i++)
            input[i] = 0;
        init(input, absolutePosition, as, Text3D.ALIGN_CENTER, null, null);
    }

    public VisualArray(int size, ArraySimulationSetting as, Vector3f translation) {
        this(size, as, Text3D.ALIGN_CENTER, null, translation);
    }

    public VisualArray(int size, ArraySimulationSetting as, int textAlignment,
                HashMap<Integer, String> mapping) {

        this(size, as, Text3D.ALIGN_CENTER, mapping, new Vector3f(0, 0, 0));
    }
```

B.5. VISUAL ARRAY

```java
    public VisualArray(Integer[] input, ArraySimulationSetting as,
                HashMap<Integer, String> mapping){
        this(input, as, Text3D.ALIGN_CENTER, mapping, new Vector3f());
    }

    public VisualArray(Integer[] input, ArraySimulationSetting as){
        this(input, as, Text3D.ALIGN_CENTER, null, new Vector3f());
    }

    public VisualArray(Integer[] input, ArraySimulationSetting as,
                Vector3f translation){
        this(input, as, Text3D.ALIGN_CENTER, null, translation);
    }

    public VisualArray(Integer[] input, Vector3f absolutePosition,
                ArraySimulationSetting as){
        this(input, absolutePosition, as, Text3D.ALIGN_CENTER, null, null);
    }

    public VisualArray(int size, ArraySimulationSetting as, int textAlignment,
                HashMap<Integer, String> mapping, Vector3f translation){
        this(size, new Vector3f(), as, textAlignment, mapping, translation);
    }

    private void init(Integer[] input, Vector3f absolutePosition,
                ArraySimulationSetting as, int textAlignment,
                HashMap<Integer, String> mapping, Vector3f translation){

        length = input.length;
        this.as = as;
        this.mapping = mapping;
        rootTG = UndoableObjectsFactory
                    .createReadWriteExtendUndoableTransformGroup();
        if (translation != null) {

            absolutePosition.add(translation);
            absolutePosition.x -= (as.fieldWidth * length) / 2f;


        }

        ComparableTransform3D transform = new ComparableTransform3D();
        transform.set(absolutePosition);

        rootTG.setTransform(transform);
        ComparableTransform3D scale = new ComparableTransform3D();
        scale.setScale(new Vector3d(1, 1, 1));

        SphereArrayField<Integer> field;
```

```java
                float startPos = 0;
                fields = new SphereArrayField[length];

                for (int i = 0; i < length; i++) {

                        field = new SphereArrayField<Integer>(this, input[i],
                        as.fieldWidth / 2, new Vector3f(startPos + i
                                        * as.fieldWidth + as.fieldWidth / 2, 0, 0), as,
                                        Text3D.ALIGN_CENTER, mapping);
                        rootTG.addChild(field);
                        fields[i] = field;

                }

                this.setCapabilities();
                this.addChild(rootTG);
                ppi = new PPI(this, as);

        }

        private VisualArray(int size, Vector3f absolutePosition,
                        ArraySimulationSetting as, int textAlignment,
                        HashMap<Integer, String> mapping, Vector3f translation) {
                Integer[] input = new Integer[size];
                for (int i = 0; i < size; i++)
        }

        public void assign(int index, ArrayField<Integer> field) {
                this.assign(index, field.getValue());
        }

        public void assignAn(int index, ArrayField<Integer> field) {
                this.assignAn(this.getField(index), field);
        }

        public void assignAn(int field1, int field2) {
                this.assignAn(this.getField(field1), this.getField(field2));
        }
        public void assignAn(ArrayField<Integer> field1, ArrayField<Integer> field2) {

                BranchGroup helpBG = new BranchGroup();
                helpBG.setCapability(BranchGroup.ALLOW_DETACH);
                TransformGroup textGroup = field2.cloneText();

                TransformGroup transformGroup = new TransformGroup();

        transformGroup.setCapability(TransformGroup.ALLOW_TRANSFORM_READ);
```

B.5. VISUAL ARRAY

```
        transformGroup.setCapability(TransformGroup.ALLOW_TRANSFORM_WRITE);

            Transform3D t = new Transform3D();
            t.setTranslation(field2.getTextAbsolutePosition());
            transformGroup.setTransform(t);

            transformGroup.addChild(textGroup);
            helpBG.addChild(transformGroup);

            Point3f p1 = new Point3f(field1.getAbsolutePosition());
            Point3f p2 = new Point3f(field2.getAbsolutePosition());

            Point3f[] positions = new Point3f[]{ p2, p1 };
            float[] knots = new float[]{ 0.0f, 1.0f };

            PositionPathInterpolator ppi = new PositionPathInterpolator(null,
                        transformGroup, new Transform3D(), knots, positions);
            ppi.setSchedulingBounds(new BoundingSphere());

            transformGroup.addChild(ppi);

            Alpha transAlpha = new Alpha(1, Math.max(100,
                        as.assign_value_increasing_alpha));

            ppi.setAlpha(transAlpha);
            this.addChild(helpBG);
            transAlpha.setStartTime(new Date().getTime());

            Navigator.startInterpolator(ppi);
            helpBG.detach();

            field1.setValue(field2.getValue());

    }
    public void assign(int index, Integer value){
            this.fields[index].setValue(value);
    }

    public void assign(ArrayField field, Integer value){
            fields[(Integer)field.getValue()].setValue(value);
    }

    public void increment(int i) {
            fields[i].setValue(fields[i].getValue() + 1);
    }

    public void decrement(int i) {
            fields[i].setValue(fields[i].getValue() - 1);
    }
```

```java
public VisualArray(Integer[] input, ArraySimulationSetting as,
            int textAlignment, HashMap<Integer, String> mapping,
            Vector3f translation){

    this(input, new Vector3f(), as, textAlignment, mapping, translation);

}
private VisualArray(Integer[] input, Vector3f absolutePosition,
            ArraySimulationSetting as, int textAlignment,
            HashMap<Integer, String> mapping, Vector3f translation){

    init(input, absolutePosition, as, textAlignment, mapping, translation);




}
private void setCapabilities(){

    this.setCapability(BranchGroup.ALLOW_DETACH);
    this.setCapability(Group.ALLOW_CHILDREN_EXTEND);
}
public ArrayField<Integer> getField(int i){
    return fields[i];
}

public Integer add(int i, int j) {
    return fields[i].getValue() + fields[j].getValue();
}

public Integer add(int i, Integer value){
    return fields[i].getValue() + value;
}

public static Integer add(ArrayField<Integer> f1, Integer value){
    return f1.getValue() + value;
}

public static Integer add(ArrayField<Integer> f1, ArrayField<Integer> f2){
    return f1.getValue() + f2.getValue();
}

public ArrayField<Integer> getField(ArrayField<Integer> field){
    return fields[field.getValue()];
}

public Integer getValue(int i){
    return fields[i].getValue();
}
```

B.5. VISUAL ARRAY

```java
public void setValue(int i, Integer value){
       fields[i].setValue(value);
}

public ArrayField<Integer> getFieldS(int i){
       highlightF(i);
       return fields[i];
}

public ArrayField<Integer> getFieldV(int i){
       highlightS(i);
       return fields[i];
}

public ArrayField<Integer> getFieldSR(int i){
       highlightP(i);
       return fields[i];
}

public void selectText(int i){
       fields[i].highlightText(as.selected_text_color);

public void highlightF(int i){
       fields[i].highlight(as.selected_field_color);

}

public void highlightF(ArrayField field){
       fields[(Integer) field.getValue()].highlight(as.selected_field_color);

}

public void highlightP(int i){
       fields[i].highlight(as.sorted_field_color);

}
public void highlightP(ArrayField field){
       field.highlight(as.sorted_field_color);

}

public void highlightS(int i){

       fields[i].highlight(as.visited_field_color);
}
public void highlightS(ArrayField field){
       field.highlight(as.visited_field_color);
}
```

```java
public void swap(int i, int j) {
        if (i == j)
                return;
        if (i < j)
                ppi.visualiseSwap(i, j);
        else
                ppi.visualiseSwap(j, i);
}
public int compare(ArrayField field1, ArrayField field2) {
        return field1.compareTo(field2);
}
public void highlightField(int i, ComparableColor3f color) {
        this.fields[i].highlight(color);
}
public void highlightSelectedField(int i) {
        this.fields[i].highlight(as.selected_field_color);
}

public void highlightSelectedFields(int... fileds_) {
        for (int i = 0; i < fileds_.length; i++)
                this.fields[fileds_[i]].highlight(as.selected_field_color);
}
public void unhighlightField(int i) {
        this.fields[i].highlight(as.default_field_color);

}
public void unhighlightField(ArrayField i) {
        this.fields[(Integer)i.getValue()].highlight(as.default_field_color);
}
public void unhighlightFields(int... fields_) {
        for (int i = 0; i < fields_.length; i++) {
                this.fields[fields_[i]].highlight(as.default_field_color);

        }
}
public void markSubArray(int i, int j) {

        if (markerTG == null) {
                this.markerTG = new UndoableBranchGroup();
                markerTG.setCapability(BranchGroup.ALLOW_DETACH);
                markerTG.setCapability(Group.ALLOW_CHILDREN_WRITE);
                markerTG.setCapability(Group.ALLOW_CHILDREN_READ);

this.markerTG.setCapability(Group.ALLOW_CHILDREN_EXTEND);
                this.rootTG.addChild(markerTG);
```

B.5. VISUAL ARRAY

```
            } else
                    markerTG.removeAllChildren();
                    ArrayMarker marker = new ArrayMarker(i, j, length, as);
                    this.markerTG.addChild(marker);

    }
    public void markField(int i) {
            this.getField(i).mark();
    }

    public void addNumber(int number) {

            SphereArrayField<Integer> field = new SphereArrayField<Integer>(this,
            number, as.fieldWidth / 2, new Vector3f(
            this.length * as.fieldWidth + as.fieldWidth / 2
                            - as.fieldWidth / 4, as.fieldWidth / 4, 0), as,
                            Text3D.ALIGN_LAST, mapping, false);
            field.setTextAppearance(SharedNodeComponents
    .createUndoableTextApperance(as.pivot_element_color));
            field.setScaleFactor(as.fieldWidth * 0.3f);
            rootTG.addChild(field);

    }
    public void removeMarker(int i) {
            this.getField(i).removeMarker();
    }
    public void removeMarker() {
            if (markerTG != null)
                    markerTG.removeAllChildren();
    }

    public VisualArray getSubArray(int from, int to) {
            Integer[] input = new Integer[to - from + 1];
            for (int i = from; i <= to; i++)
                    input[i] = this.getValue(i);
            return new VisualArray(input, as);
    }

    public VisualArray getSubArray(int from, int to, Vector3f absolutPoistion) {

            Integer[] input = new Integer[to - from + 1];
            for (int i = from, j = 0; i <= to; i++)
                    input[j++] = this.getValue(i);
            return new VisualArray(input, absolutPoistion, as);

    }

    public int findMin(int i) {
            int min = i;
            this.markSubArray(i, length - 1);
            this.highlightField(min, as.found_field_color);
```

```java
            for (int j = i + 1; j < length; j++) {
                    this.highlightField(j, as.selected_field_color);
                    Navigator.sleep(as.highlight_delay);
                    if (fields[min].compareTo(this.getField(j)) > 0) {

                            this.unhighlightField(min);
                            min = j;
                            this.highlightField(min, as.found_field_color);

                            Navigator.sleep(as.highlight_delay);
                    }

                    this.unhighlightField(j);
                    this.highlightField(min, as.found_field_color);

            }

            this.highlightField(min, as.found_field_color);
            this.removeMarker();
            return min;
    }

    public void split(int i) {
            float dx = as.fieldWidth / 8;
            for (int j = 0; j < i; j++) {
                    Vector3d translation = this.fields[j].getTranslation();
                    translation.x -= dx;
                    this.fields[j].setTranslation(translation);

            }
            for (int j = i; j < fields.length; j++) {
                    Vector3d translation = this.fields[j].getTranslation();
                    translation.x += dx;
                    this.fields[j].setTranslation(translation);
            }
    }

    @Override
    public void addChild(Node child) {

            super.addChild(child);
    }

    public void addRightArrow() {
            Vector3f translation = new Vector3f();

            translation.y += 3 * 2 * as.fieldWidth / 10 + as.fieldHight / 4;
            if (length > 1)
             translation.x += ((length) / 2.f) * as.fieldWidth - as.fieldWidth / 2;
```

B.5. VISUAL ARRAY

```
                Arrow bg = new Arrow(as.fieldWidth / 10, 2 * as.fieldWidth / 10,
                            as.arrowColor, translation, Math.PI / 4);
                this.rootTG.addChild(bg);

        }

        public void addLeftArrow(){

                Vector3f translation = new Vector3f();
                translation.y += 3 * 2 * as.fieldWidth / 10 + as.fieldHight / 4;
                if (length > 1)
                        translation.x += (length / 2.f) * as.fieldWidth + as.fieldWidth / 2;
                else
                        translation.x += as.fieldWidth;
                this.rootTG.addChild(new Arrow(as.fieldWidth / 10,
                            2 * as.fieldWidth / 10, as.arrowColor, translation,
                            -Math.PI / 4));

        }

        public void unhighlightArrows(){
                Enumeration<Node> en = this.rootTG.getAllChildren();
                while (en.hasMoreElements()){
                        Node next = en.nextElement();
                        if (next instanceof Arrow){
                                Arrow arrow = (Arrow) next;
arrow.cone.getAppearance().getMaterial().setDiffuseColor(
                                            as.unhighlitedArrowColor);

arrow.cone.getAppearance().getMaterial().setAmbientColor(
                                            as.unhighlitedArrowColor);
                        }
                }
        }
        public ArrayField cloneField(int i){
                ArrayField field = this.getField(i);

                ArrayField f = new SphereArrayField(null, field.getValue(), field
                            .getWidth() / 2, field.getAbsolutePosition(), as, field
                            .getTextAlignment(), field.getMapping(),
field.createSphere());
                f.setAppearance(field.getApperance());
                return f;
        }

        public ArrayField cloneFieldAn(int i){
                ArrayField field = this.getField(i);

                ArrayField f = new SphereArrayField(null, field.getValue(), field
                            .getWidth() / 2, field.getAbsolutePosition(), as, field
                            .getTextAlignment(), field.getMapping(),
```

184 APPENDIX B. SOURCE CODE LISTINGS

```
            field.createSphere());
            f.setAppearance(field.getApperance());
            Vector3f to = field.getAbsolutePosition();
            to.add(new Vector3f(0, as.y_translation, 0));
            this.addChild((Node)f);
            ppi.moveAnimated(f, to);
            return f;
    }

    public void translate(Vector3f translation) {

            ComparableTransform3D tTrans = new ComparableTransform3D();
            rootTG.getTransform(tTrans);
            Vector3f absolutePosition = new Vector3f();
            tTrans.get(absolutePosition);
            translation.add(absolutePosition);
            tTrans.set(translation);
            rootTG.setTransform(tTrans);

    }

    public Vector3f getAbsolutePosition() {
            ComparableTransform3D tTrans = new ComparableTransform3D();
            rootTG.getTransform(tTrans);
            Vector3f absolutePosition = new Vector3f();
            tTrans.get(absolutePosition);

            return absolutePosition;

    }

    public void addAdditionalText(int i, String text) {

            this.fields[i].addAdditionalText(text);
    }

    public void removeAdditionalText(int i) {
            this.fields[i].removeAdditionalText();
    }
}
```

Listing B.5: Implemenation of an array as a visual object

B.6 Undo/Redo Snapshot

```
                         Undo Redo Snapshot
/**
 * 3D-VISIAN-Project http://www.3dvisian.de
 * @3DVISIAN (#) visian3d.undo.Snapshot.java
 * Created on 12.05.2008
 * Copyright (c) 2007-2009, Inc. All Rights Reserved.
 * Goethe-Universität Frankfurt/Main, Department of Computer Science and Mathematics,
 * Institute of Computer Graphics (Prof. Dr. Detlef Krömker)
 * http://www.gdv.informatik.uni-frankfurt.de
 *
 * @author Ashraf Abu Baker
 * @version 1.0
 */
package visian3d.undo;

import java.util.Enumeration;
import java.util.HashMap;
import java.util.LinkedHashMap;

import javax.media.j3d.Appearance;
import javax.media.j3d.Geometry;
import javax.media.j3d.Group;
import javax.media.j3d.Node;
import javax.media.j3d.Shape3D;
```

```java
public class Snapshot {

    private final int snapshotID;
    public Integer sceneHashKey;
    private IUndoableBranchGroup scene;
    private HashMap<Integer, IUndoableBranchGroup> undoableBGs = new HashMap<Integer,
            IUndoableBranchGroup>();
    private HashMap<Integer, IUndoableTransformGroup> undoableTGs = new HashMap<Integer,
            IUndoableTransformGroup>();

    private HashMap<Integer, IUndoableNode> undoableNodes = new HashMap<Integer,
            IUndoableNode>();
    private HashMap<Integer, Node> nonUndoableNodes = new HashMap<Integer, Node>();
    public HashMap<Integer, LinkedHashMap<Integer, Integer>> keys = new HashMap<Integer,
            LinkedHashMap<Integer, Integer>>();

    public Snapshot(IUndoableBranchGroup group, int snapshotID) {
            this.snapshotID = snapshotID;
            this.scene = group;
            takeSnapshot();
    }

    private void takeSnapshot() {

            sceneHashKey = scene.getHashKey();

            takeSnapshotOfUGroup(scene, 0);

    }

    private void takeSnapshotOfUGroup(IUndoableGroup group, int depth) {

            group.takeSnapshot(snapshotID);
            int groupKey = group.getHashKey();

            Enumeration<Node> children = group.getAllChildren();

            LinkedHashMap<Integer, Integer>
            keyOrHashKeyOfEachChildAndItsCorrespondingNodeType =
            new LinkedHashMap<Integer, Integer>();

                while (children.hasMoreElements()) {
                        Node childNode = children.nextElement();

                        if ((childNode instanceof IUndoableNode)) {
```

B.6. UNDO/REDO SNAPSHOT

```
                        IUndoableNode child = (IUndoableNode) childNode;

                        Integer key = child.getHashKey();
                        int type = child.getType();

       keyOrHashKeyOfEachChildAndItsCorrespondingNodeType.put(key,
                                                 type);
                        switch (type) {

                        case IUndoableNode.BRANCH_GROUP:

                        undoableBGs.put(key, (IUndoableBranchGroup) child);
                        takeSnapshotOfUGroup((IUndoableBranchGroup) child,
                                                 depth+1);
                                break;

                        case IUndoableNode.TRANSFORM_GROUP:

                        undoableTGs.put(key, (IUndoableTransformGroup) child);
                        takeSnapshotOfUGroup((IUndoableTransformGroup) child,
                                                 depth+1);
                                break;

                        default:
                                undoableNodes.put(key, child);
                                takeSnapshotOfUNode(child, depth+1);

                        }

                }
                else {

                        Integer key = childNode.hashCode();

                        nonUndoableNodes.put(key, childNode);

               keyOrHashKeyOfEachChildAndItsCorrespondingNodeType.put(key,
                                        IUndoableNode.NON_UNDOABLE);

                        if (childNode instanceof Group)
                                takeSnapshotOfGroup((Group) childNode, depth);
                        else
                                apshotOfNode(childNode, depth);

                }
        }
        keys.put(groupKey,
  keyOrHashKeyOfEachChildAndItsCorrespondingNodeType);

   }
```

```java
        }

        private void takeSnapshotOfUNode(IUndoableNode node, int depth) {

                node.takeSnapshot(snapshotID);

        }

        private void takeSnapshotOfNode(Node node, int depth) {

                if (node instanceof Shape3D) {
                        Shape3D shape = (Shape3D) node;
                        Appearance app = shape.getAppearance();
                        if (app instanceof IUndoableObject)
                                ((IUndoableObject) app).takeSnapshot(snapshotID);
                        Geometry geo = shape.getGeometry();
                        if (geo instanceof IUndoableObject)
                                ((IUndoableObject) geo).takeSnapshot(snapshotID);
                }

        }

        private void takeSnapshotOfGroup(Group group, int depth) {

                Enumeration<Node> children = group.getAllChildren();
                while (children.hasMoreElements()) {
                        Node childNode = children.nextElement();
                    if (childNode instanceof IUndoableNode)
                        if (childNode instanceof IUndoableGroup)
                          takeSnapshotOfUGroup((IUndoableGroup) childNode, depth + 1);
                            else
                          takeSnapshotOfUNode((IUndoableNode) childNode, depth + 1);
                        else if (childNode instanceof Group)
                                takeSnapshotOfGroup((Group) childNode, depth + 1);
                        else
                                takeSnapshotOfNode(childNode, depth + 1);
                }

        }

        public IUndoableBranchGroup reconstructScene() {

                scene.detach();
                reconstructUGroup(scene);
                return scene;

        }

        private void reconstructGroup(Group group) {

                Enumeration<Node> children = group.getAllChildren();
```

B.6. UNDO/REDO SNAPSHOT

```
                    case IUndoableNode.NON_UNDOABLE:

                            Node otherChild = nonUndoableNodes.get(child);

                            uGroup.addChild(otherChild);

                            if (otherChild instanceof Group)
                                    reconstructGroup((Group) otherChild);
                            else
                                    reconstructNode(otherChild);
                            break;

                    case IUndoableNode.BRANCH_GROUP:

                            IUndoableBranchGroup bgChild = undoableBGs.get(child);

                            bgChild.detach();
                            uGroup.addChild((UndoableBranchGroup) bgChild);
                            reconstructUGroup(bgChild);
                            break;

                    case IUndoableNode.TRANSFORM_GROUP:

                            IUndoableTransformGroup tgChild = undoableTGs.get(child);

                            uGroup.addChild((UndoableTransformGroup) tgChild);
                            reconstructUGroup(tgChild);

                            break;

                    default:

                            IUndoableNode hashChild = undoableNodes.get(child);

                            uGroup.addChild((Node) hashChild);
                            reconstructUNode(hashChild);
                            break;
                    }
            }
        }
    }
}
```

Listing B.6: Undo/Redo snapshot

Appendix C

Miscellaneous

C.1   Java 3D

The Java 3D API is a high-level, scene graph-based API consisting of a hierarchical collection of Java classes which serve as an interface for developing platform-independent three-dimensional applications. A Java 3D programme is mainly assembled from geometrical primitives, appearance and behaviour objects. A geometrical object describes the structure of a visual object. An appearance object describes what a visual object should look like when it is rendered. Behaviour objects are used to add animation behaviour to virtual scenes. The objects of a Java 3D programme are arranged in a so-called scene graph. A scene graph is a tree structure that arranges the logical and often (but not necessarily) the spatial depiction of a 3D scene. It completely specifies the content of a virtual scene, and how it is to be rendered.

The nodes and arcs of the scene graph represent Java 3D objects and the relationships between these objects, respectively. There are two types of nodes: group nodes and leaf nodes [119]. Leaf nodes are usually used to hold visual, behaviour, or lighting objects. Group objects are used to arrange scene graph objects into groups. There is also a third sort of Java 3D objects, called *NodeComponent*. According to the Java 3D specification [68], *NodeComponents* do not belong to the scene graph tree and are not scene graph objects. They can, however, be referenced by the scene graph and used, for example, to define the geometry and appearance attributes of visual objects. It is at this point important to emphasise, that a scene graph is actually a tree and not a graph.

The root of a scene graph is a *Locale* object which represents the coordinate systems of the virtual scene. There are two relevant terms that are frequently used in the Java 3D terminology: live and compiled. Adding a group object, particularly a *BranchGroup* (see below), to a *Locale* makes the group and all of its ancestors live. Live objects are subject to being rendered. The parameters of live objects cannot be modified unless the corresponding flags (capabilities) have been explicitly set before the object became live. The same applies to compiled objects. Compiling a group object converts it and all of its ancestors into a more efficient internal representation for rendering. Many Java 3D objects have 'capabilities'. A capability is a flag that specifies whether or not the object can be accessed and, if so, in which way. Capabilities are a powerful feature for increasing the performance of Java 3D applications. The most important group classes of Java 3D are *BranchGroup* and *TransformGroup* [119]. Instances of *BranchGroups* are used to define the structure of the scene graph. They are the only objects allowed to be children of *Locale* objects and can have multiple children. The children of a *BranchGroup* object can be other groups or leaf objects, such as shape objects (which are intrinsically visual objects). *TransformGroup* objects hold geometric transformations, such as translations and rotations. A transformation is typically specified in a *Transform3D* object, which is, like a *NodeComponent*, not a scene graph object. In a 3D scene, each 3D object of an application either resides in the scene graph, in which case it is called a scene graph object, or it is referenced by one or several scene graph objects, as is the case with *NodeComponents* [68, 119]. In both cases each 3D object is reachable from the root of the graph. To learn more about Java 3D refer to the following book [108].

Die VDM Verlagsservicegesellschaft sucht für wissenschaftliche Verlage abgeschlossene und herausragende

Dissertationen, Habilitationen, Diplomarbeiten, Master Theses, Magisterarbeiten usw.

für die kostenlose Publikation als Fachbuch.

Sie verfügen über eine Arbeit, die hohen inhaltlichen und formalen Ansprüchen genügt, und haben Interesse an einer honorarvergüteten Publikation?

Dann senden Sie bitte erste Informationen über sich und Ihre Arbeit per Email an *info@vdm-vsg.de*.

Sie erhalten kurzfristig unser Feedback!

VDM Verlagsservicegesellschaft mbH
Dudweiler Landstr. 99   Telefon +49 681 3720 174
D - 66123 Saarbrücken   Fax   +49 681 3720 1749

www.vdm-vsg.de

Die VDM Verlagsservicegesellschaft mbH vertritt

Printed by Books on Demand GmbH, Norderstedt / Germany